The Chamberlain Sampler of
AMERICAN COOKING

The
Chamberlain Sampler
of
AMERICAN
COOKING

in Recipes and Pictures

By NARCISSE CHAMBERLAIN

and NARCISSA G. CHAMBERLAIN

Photographs by Samuel Chamberlain

HASTINGS HOUSE, *Publishers*, NEW YORK 22

Published simultaneously in Canada
by S. J. Reginald Saunders, Publishers, Toronto 2B.

Library of Congress Catalog Card Number: 61–14217
Printed in the United States of America

Introduction

❧

This sampler of American recipes represents the authors' personal idea of good food in America today; we have given book room only to our preferences. We've been equally personal about our bird's-eye view of the national scene, which includes only photographs of America as we prefer to look at it.

The variety we had to choose from proved to be staggering. If you want cookbooks that survey the whole scope of American regional, traditional, and present-day cooking on an encyclopedic scale, there are a dozen or so current ones that try and heaven knows how many that deal in one specialty or another. They are collectively fascinating, full of excellent as well as thoroughly pedestrian dishes, and so choked with information you can't see the forest for the recipes.

American cooking has been deservedly maligned at times. Whoever first decreed that the maraschino cherry is a legitimate ingredient of a salad surely brought us, in cooperation with the one who added diced marshmallows, to the brink of national disgrace. There are still foreigners who think that these delicacies, plus a praiseworthy but endless series of steaks and coconut layer cakes, pretty much symbolise the level of imagination in the U.S. kitchen.

This is simply not true, but the wrong impression is understandable. There are enough standardized, not-very-good restaurants across the country positively to promote it for the poorly guided visitor. Much more interesting is the obstacle of sheer numbers of kitchen traditions that flourish simultaneously yet somehow separately from coast to coast. This accumulation is the cardinal virtue of American cooking, though even Americans are not all aware of it. As a visit to New York City is not a visit to all America, so a session with Fanny Farmer, bless her indispensable book, will not tell you 90 percent of what our good cooks have to offer.

You'll never find that 90 percent represented in any one restaurant, any one book, or any one home kitchen. But if you consult enough cooks, cookbooks, and just plain people who like to eat well, you discover that America, over-all, is astonishingly open-minded about cooking. By way of contrast, for instance, it is a rare French cook who could be persuaded to adopt a Korean recipe for chicken as Californians do, or to make a Brazilian dessert with avocados as a New England friend of ours does. French cooks singlemindedly cook dishes that are French, which admittedly does give them plenty to choose from. But American cooks have for generations drawn on the contributions of their European mother countries, of a fair share of Asia, not to speak of Fanny Farmer, the American Indian, the innately talented Southern Negro cook, or the now ubiquitous modern food editor.

Small wonder the culinary situation is a bit of a hodge-podge, but let no one say American cooking is limited. At worst it has only fallen on occasional unhappy days, as in the years between the two wars when the percentage of uninspired cooks is supposed to have reached an all-time high. Prohibition and marshmallows in the salad both date from these curious times; maybe there is some sinister connection. But history shook up the whole world at the end of that era and, if you view history for a moment from the vantage point of the dinner table, it occurs to you that steak-and-potatoes isolationism declined in almost direct proportion to the decline of isolationism in American politics. A heady hypothesis for anyone who cares to pursue it but, nevertheless, foreign food did begin to invade our kitchens with a vengeance a couple of decades ago. And with it came also a popular rage for recipes in general, which meant American regional recipes too, both new and old. The enthusiasm may at length have been ever so slightly tainted with commercialism, but they're selling Connecticut Rock Cornish game hens in Missouri now, and serving Polynesian concoctions in Boston, and the customers quite rightly love it.

If you like to collect recipes, as we do, it quickly turns out that the file headed "American" is by far the most various. It will not hark back to a firm central tradition such as made French cuisine great, nor have the perfected subtleties of the Chinese, or the consistent styles that identify the Italian or Scandinavian. The sensible, well-made recipes referred to as plain American food are the only ones that are common to the whole country and they are only a fraction of the national kitchen lore. This, for sheer diversity, can be matched by the cooking of no other country in the Western world. To mention but a handful of classic examples, Texas chili, boiled beef, steak and kidney pie, cheese blintzes, butterfly shrimp, or beef Stroganoff are all as American as Indian pudding or baking-powder biscuits by now. Yet any cook but an American one would consider this an international collection.

It is this wonderful variety that has charmed us—and that has led to the enormous tomes of American cookery which nowadays are being written by the large staffs of large magazines because no one person can cope with them. We have concluded that this particular quality of American cooking can be communicated in a nutshell almost better than in a 10-pound book. At any rate, a little book need only contain what we like best, albeit a part only of that, too.

In the same vein, it is a pleasure to give photographs of Georgian architecture precedence over those of industry, to let New England valleys outnumber skyscrapers, to have the picturesque override the portrait of mass civilization which might have been more representative of the facts. But then, the facts are, also, that ready-mix cakes have come to outnumber real ones. So why go into all of that? Everyone still loves a good recipe or a gratifyingly nostalgic landscape. And it is no accident that the food and the buildings and the open vistas have an almost equal diversity. The people and the soil contrive together to do this in any country. The wonder is only that, in a nation of such well-known contrasts, the originality of its best native dishes should come to anyone as a surprise.

NARCISSE CHAMBERLAIN

Contents

❦

List of Illustrations

❧

Acknowledgments

❧

*This book was illustrated with the generous cooperation
of the following photographers and organizations:*

Alabama State Chamber of Commerce, 123

American Airlines, 66, 67

Arizona Development Board, 158, 197

Bacon, William A., 79

Chamberlain, Samuel, 2, 11, 17, 23, 30, 31, 38, 40, 43, 45, 51, 54, 62, 68, 70, 76, 77, 78, 83, 86, 89, 94, 97, 98, 107, 112, 113, 114, 115, 120, 130, 132, 137, 162, 168, 175, 177, 180, 185, 191, 196, 198, 200, 202, 203, 206, 208, 209, 215

Cities Service Company, 4, 39, 46, 59, 71

Colorado State Advertising & Publicity Dept., 90, 125

Delaware Chamber of Commerce, 116

Delaware State Development Dept., 214

Devaney, A., 9, 48, 53, 55, 72, 103, 135, 148, 150, 153, 159, 160, 163, 164. 165, 166, 179, 181, 188, 195, 213, 216

Florida Development Commission, 82, 161

Florida State News Bureau, 88

Galloway, Ewing, 8, 16, 21, 33, 36, 56, 60, 64, 145, 155, 199

Great Northern Railway, 176

Hatcher, Thurston, 25, 172

Henle, Fritz, 4

Iowa Development Commission, 84

Kansas Industrial Development Commission, 96

Kuhlman, Mrs. Harold, 29

Lowman, Hubert A., 35, 61

Maryland Department of Information, 193

Miami, City of, News Bureau, 74, 108, 122

Miller, Martin H., 69, 201

Missouri Resources Division, 140

Montana Chamber of Commerce, 93, 151, 173, 174

Nevada State Highway Department, 117, 149

New Mexico State Tourist Bureau, 110, 138, 204

New York State Dept. of Commerce, 144, 152, 170

THE STATUE OF LIBERTY   *New York Harbor*

Lobster Thermidor

(Lobster, mushrooms, brandy, milk, cream, broth, egg yolks, mustard, Parmesan)

In a skillet heat 3 cups of diced cooked lobster meat in 4 tablespoons of melted butter. Stir often and do not brown. In another skillet sauté ½ pound of sliced mushrooms in 2 tablespoons of butter for 3 or 4 minutes. When the lobster is hot, add ¼ cup of warmed brandy, light it, and shake the pan until the flame dies. Remove the lobster and blend 2 tablespoons of flour into the juices left in the skillet. Add gradually ½ cup each of milk, cream, and clear chicken broth, and simmer the sauce, stirring often, until it is slightly thickened. Add 2 egg yolks mixed with another ½ cup of cream, 1 teaspoon of dry mustard, and salt and pepper to taste. Thicken the sauce over low heat, stirring constantly, and without letting it boil, then add the lobster and mushrooms. Transfer the mixture to lobster shells if you started with whole boiled lobsters, or to six ramekins. Sprinkle with bread crumbs and Parmesan cheese, dot with butter, and brown in a 375° oven for 10 minutes. Serves six.

1

YALE UNIVERSITY
New Haven, Connecticut

Samuel Chamberlain

Yale Beets

(Beets, cornstarch, sugar, orange juice, lemon juice, butter)

Peel and slice thinly 12 medium-sized boiled beets. Arrange the slices in a buttered baking dish and over them pour ½ cup of orange juice mixed with 1 tablespoon of cornstarch, ½ teaspoon of salt, ⅛ teaspoon of pepper, 2 tablespoons of sugar and 1 tablespoon of lemon juice. Dot the beets generously with butter and bake them, tightly covered, in a 400° oven for ½ hour, stirring them once or twice. Serves six.

THE CAPITOL
Washington, D. C.

Union Pacific Railroad

U.S. SENATE BEAN SOUP

(White beans, ham bone, onions, celery, potatoes, garlic, parsley)

Soak 1 pound of dried white beans overnight in water to cover. Drain them and put them in a soup kettle with a ham bone that has some generous scraps of meat left on it and 3 quarts of water. Bring the water to a boil and simmer the beans, covered, for 2 hours. Then add 3 onions and 3 stalks of celery (including the tops), all finely chopped, 1 cup of mashed potatoes, 2 minced cloves of garlic, and ¼ cup of chopped parsley. Simmer the soup for another hour and taste it for seasoning. Remove the ham bone, dice the meat from it and put the ham back in the soup. Serves four for a one-dish supper, six to eight otherwise.

3

OIL DERRICK AND COWBOYS AT SUNSET   *Texas*

BROILED ONIONS

(Spanish onions, butter, salt, pepper)

Peel large sweet Spanish onions, cut them in ¼-inch-thick slices, and spread them out in a large shallow roasting pan. Sprinkle them with salt and plenty of freshly ground pepper, and douse them generously with melted butter. Broil them under a high flame, turning them once or twice, until they are cooked and well-browned but still slightly crisp in the center. These are better than fried onions and will transform an ordinary hamburger into a feast. For broiled steak and liver, too, of course.

4

THE SAN ANTONIO RIVER   *San Antonio, Texas*

CREAM OF AVOCADO SOUP

(Avocados, chicken soup, onion, cream, cayenne, chives)

Force the meat of 1½ large ripe avocados through a fine sieve. Add 2 cups of hot clear chicken soup and 1 teaspoon of grated onion, bring the mixture to a boil and add 1 cup of heavy cream. Season to taste with salt, white pepper, and a little chili powder, and serve very hot, with a few cubes of chilled avocado in each serving, and with a sprinkling of minced fresh chives. Serves six.

UPSTATE FARM
near Cooperstown, New York

Standard Oil Company

Cheddar Dollars

(Cheddar cheese, butter, flour, cayenne pepper)

Grate ½ pound of aged, sharp Cheddar cheese and cream it very thoroughly with ¼ pound of butter and 1 cup of flour. Season the dough with ½ teaspoon of salt and a hint of cayenne pepper, and roll it into a long sausage shape about 1 inch in diameter. Wrap the roll in aluminum foil and chill it thoroughly. To bake the dollars, cut the roll into slices ⅛ of an inch thick, spread them on a cookie sheet and put them in a 350° oven just long enough to turn them pale gold. Never let them brown. You can either bake the whole batch and store the dollars, which keep very well, in a tightly covered jar; or you can keep the uncooked roll in the refrigerator, slice it off as you need it and serve the dollars hot, fresh from the oven.

6

ORANGE GROVES BELOW MT. SAN GORGONIO   *Union Pacific Railroad*
near Redlands, California

Orange Barbecued Duck

(Duck, oranges, chicken stock, port, currant jelly, lemon juice, ginger, cayenne)

To serve four people, rub a 6-pound duck lightly inside and out with salt and pepper. For an outdoor barbecue, roast it on an electric spit; or roast it in a 325° oven, allowing about 25 minutes per pound. Prick the skin thoroughly to allow the excess fat to run off, and baste the duck several times with a half-and-half mixture of orange juice and chicken stock or consommé. Serve the duck with the following barbecue sauce:

Peel the orange zest from the skin of half an orange, cut it in slivers, simmer it for 3 minutes in a little water, and drain it. Skim the fat from the juices left in the roasting pan and add to them the orange zest, 1 cup of orange juice, ¼ cup of port, ¼ cup of currant jelly, 3 tablespoons of lemon juice, ¼ teaspoon of powdered ginger, and cayenne pepper, black pepper and salt to taste. Simmer the sauce while the duck is being carved and serve immediately.

7

BUCKINGHAM MEMORIAL FOUNTAIN
Chicago, Illinois

Ewing Galloway

Planked Lake Michigan Whitefish

(Lake Michigan whitefish, butter, lemon, parsley, mashed potatoes)

Split a 3½- to 4-pound Lake Michigan whitefish and remove the backbone. Preheat a hardwood plank about 2 inches thick by pouring boiling water over it. Lay the fish flat on the plank, skin-side down. Season it well with salt and white pepper and dot it generously with butter. Bake the fish in a 450° oven for 20 minutes and baste it 4 or 5 times with a few spoonfuls of mixed hot water, melted butter and lemon juice. Then take the plank out of the oven and make a ring of mashed potatoes, beaten fluffy with plenty of cream and butter, around the fish. Return the plank to the oven for about 5 minutes, or until the whitefish is done and the potatoes are golden brown. Serve from the plank, with a sauce made of ¾ cup of melted butter, 2 tablespoons of minced parsley and 2 tablespoons of lemon juice. Serves six.

THE MITCHELL HOUSE
Mobile, Alabama

A. Devaney

Alabama Fried Chicken

(Chicken, white corn meal, flour, shortening, cream)

Cut a young chicken into small serving pieces. Run water over the chicken, drain it, season the pieces with salt and pepper and roll them in a half-and-half mixture of white corn meal and flour. Heat melted shortening a half inch deep in a large iron skillet. When the fat is hot enough to spit at a drop of water, arrange all the largest pieces on the bottom of the skillet and put the last pieces on top.

Brown the bottom layer of chicken over a medium flame, turn the pieces to brown them on the other side, then shift the smaller pieces to the bottom of the skillet. When all the pieces are brown on all sides, add ¼ cup of water, lower the flame, cover the skillet and let the chicken cook through. The total cooking time should be about 35 minutes.

Remove the chicken to a hot platter and keep it warm. Pour any excess fat out of the skillet, but keep the brown pieces that have crumbled off the chicken. Melt 1 tablespoon of butter in the skillet and blend in 2 teaspoons of flour. Add gradually 1 cup of light cream, stir the gravy until it thickens and season it with salt, plenty of pepper and a pinch of mace. Serve the cream gravy separately. Serves three; for six, fry 2 chickens in separate skillets.

9

LOST RIVER VALLEY   *Standard Oil Company*
near Mackay, Idaho

SOUR CREAM AND CHIVES BAKED POTATOES

(Idaho potatoes, butter, sour cream, chives)

Bake large Idaho potatoes in a 400° oven for 50 minutes or more, until the centers are soft. Slit the tops lengthwise, pinch the potatoes open and put a little salt and pepper and a generous lump of butter in each one. Spread each opening with a big spoonful of sour cream, sprinkle the cream with minced chives and serve the potatoes immediately. Be sure to have extra butter, sour cream and chives on the table.

OLD SEAPORT STREET
Mystic, Connecticut

Samuel Chamberlain

Braised Rock Cornish Game Birds

(Rock Cornish game birds, onion, butter, bread crumbs, nut meats, herbs, white wine)

In a skillet sauté 1 minced onion in 3 tablespoons of butter until it is soft. Remove the skillet from the fire and add 1 cup of toasted bread crumbs, ½ cup of chopped nut meats, ½ teaspoon of poultry seasoning, 1 tablespoon of chopped parsley, and salt and pepper. Moisten the stuffing with 2 or 3 tablespoons of white wine or chicken consommé and with it half-fill the cavities of 6 dressed Rock Cornish game birds weighing about 1¼ pounds each. Truss the birds loosely and put them in a large Dutch oven. Put ½ slice of bacon over the breast of each one, add 1 cup of dry white wine or chicken consommé, cover the Dutch oven and cook the birds in a 450° oven for 45 minutes. Then transfer them to an ovenproof serving dish, discard the bacon, dot the birds lightly with butter and brown them briefly under the broiler flame. Skim most of the fat from the juices in the Dutch oven, reduce the sauce over a brisk flame, and serve it in a sauceboat.

11

GROUND PATTERN NEAR LINWOOD, KANSAS   *Standard Oil Company*

Green Tomato Pickle

(Green tomatoes, onions, cider vinegar, brown sugar, peppers, garlic, spices)

Wash and slice thinly 6 pounds of green tomatoes. Peel and slice thinly 6 large onions. Sprinkle the vegetables with ½ cup of common salt and let them stand overnight in an earthenware bowl or crock. The next day, rinse them in cold water and drain them.

In an enamel kettle mix 6 cups of cider vinegar with 2 pounds of brown sugar. Add 6 green peppers and 3 sweet red peppers, all seeded, stemmed and diced, and 6 minced cloves of garlic. Bring the mixture to a boil and add the tomatoes and onions, 1 tablespoon of whole cloves, a 2-inch piece of stick cinnamon, 1 tablespoon of powdered ginger, 1 tablespoon of dry mustard, 1 tablespoon of celery seed and 1 heaping teaspoon of salt. Simmer the pickle for 1 hour, stirring often, ladle it into hot sterilized jars and seal them immediately.

OAKLAND BAY BRIDGE   *Santa Fe Railway*
San Francisco, California

Eggs Foo Yung

(Eggs, scallions, crab meat, water chestnuts, bean sprouts, soy sauce)

In a skillet sauté 6 chopped scallions in 2 tablespoons of butter until they are soft but not brown. Take the skillet off the fire and add ¾ cup of crab meat, ½ cup of sliced water chestnuts (or button mushrooms if you cannot get the chestnuts), and 1½ cups of bean sprouts (thoroughly drained if you must use canned ones). Season the mixture with 2 teaspoons of soy sauce. In a bowl beat 8 eggs with ¾ cup of water and mix in the vegetables and crab meat. Make 6 separate omelettes in a small pan with this batter, turning them once to cook them golden-brown, but not too brown, on both sides. Heat 1 teaspoon of oil in the pan before starting each omelette.

Serve the eggs foo yung with a little very hot mustard, and with a clear Chinese sauce made with 1 cup of chicken consommé seasoned with ¾ teaspoon of sugar and 1 teaspoon of soy sauce and thickened with 2½ teaspoons of cornstarch first dissolved in a spoonful of the consommé. Serves six.

THE CHUCK WAGON
Andrews County, Texas

Standard Oil Company

Texas Chili Con Carne (with beans)

(Pinto beans, beef suet, onion, garlic, beef, tomatoes, chili, cumin)

Soak 2 cups of pink or pinto beans in water overnight. The next morning, drain them, cover them with fresh water, and simmer them gently until they are almost tender.

Melt 3 tablespoons of chopped beef suet in a deep, heavy pot and add 1 large chopped onion and 2 minced cloves of garlic. When the onion begins to brown, add 1 pound of lean beef, cut in ½-inch cubes, and brown the meat quickly to seal in the juices. Blend 1 tablespoon of flour and add 2½ cups of Italian plum tomatoes and 1 cup of the water in which the beans were cooked. Add 1 teaspoon of salt, 1 to 3 tablespoons of chili powder to taste (or 2 to 4 ground chili peppers), and ½ teaspoon of ground cumin. Simmer the chili, covered, for 1 hour; then mix in the beans, drained, and taste for seasoning. Cook the chili for another 30 minutes, stirring occasionally, but do not let the beans get soft or broken.

Chili con carne, like a good stew, improves in flavor if it is set aside for about 12 hours and is reheated before serving. Serves four to six.

14

TELEGRAPH HILL
San Francisco, California

Union Pacific Railroad

Chinese Stuffed Lobster with Pork

(Lobster, cooked pork, ginger, garlic, chicken consommé, soy sauce)

Split three 2-pound boiled lobsters down the center, remove all the meat and save the shells. Cut the lobster meat in chunks and sauté them briefly in 3 tablespoons of salad oil without letting them brown. Mix together 1½ pounds of cooked pork, cut in very thin strips, 3 tablespoons of minced candied ginger (or fresh green ginger if you can get it), and 3 small mashed cloves of garlic. Add the lobster meat, stuff the lobster shells with the mixture and arrange them in a large casserole. Pour hot, clear chicken consommé about 1 inch deep in the bottom of the casserole. Simmer the lobsters, covered, over a low flame for 30 minutes, basting them occasionally with the consommé. Transfer the lobsters to a deep serving platter. Thicken 1½ cups of the juice in the casserole with 4 teaspoons of cornstarch first dissolved in a little water, season it with soy sauce and pour it over the lobsters. Serves six.

15

FARM LANDS
Sheboygan County, Wisconsin

Ewing Galloway

Ham Steaks and Cranberries

(Ham steaks, cranberries, honey, cloves)

Mix 2 cups of raw split cranberries with 1 cup of honey. Place a 1-inch-thick slice of ham in a baking dish and spread it with half the cranberries. Insert half a dozen whole cloves around the edge of a second slice of ham, put it on top of the first slice, and spread it with the rest of the berries. Cover the baking dish and bake the ham in a 350° oven for 1½ hours, basting it several times with the pan juices. Serves six.

THE BIRTHPLACE OF CALVIN COOLIDGE   *Samuel Chamberlain*
Plymouth, Vermont

Vermont Baked Apples

(Apples, seedless raisins, butter, maple syrup, lemon juice)

Wash 6 large, firm apples, core them without cutting through the stem ends, pare them one third of the way down on the cored end, and arrange them in a shallow baking dish. In the hollow of each apple put a few seedless raisins and 1 teaspoon of butter. Sprinkle the apples with the juice of ½ a lemon and over them pour 1 cup of Vermont maple syrup mixed with ⅓ cup of water. Bake them in a 400° oven for about 45 minutes, or until they are cooked through. Be sure to baste the apples with the pan juices at least 5 or 6 times as they cook. Serve them hot with a pitcher of heavy cream.

17

FARMLAND NEAR HUSBAND, PENNSYLVANIA   *Standard Oil Company*

Hot Potato Salad

(New potatoes, sweet onion, sweet pepper, fresh dill, French dressing)

Wash 2 pounds of new potatoes and boil them in their jackets in water to cover. Drain them when they are tender but before many of the skins break. Peel and slice the potatoes and sprinkle them with 1 sweet onion and 1 sweet pepper, both finely diced, and 3 tablespoons of chopped fresh dill. Toss the salad very gently with a French dressing made of 3 tablespoons of vinegar, 8 tablespoons of salad oil, and salt, pepper and prepared mustard to taste. Serve the potato salad immediately, or keep it warm in the top of a double boiler until servingtime. Serves six.

THE COUNTY COURTHOUSE
Mount Holly, New Jersey

Standard Oil Company

Chocolate Icebox Mousse

(Unsalted butter, powdered sugar, eggs, chocolate, brandy)

With a wooden spoon cream thoroughly ¼ pound of unsalted butter and beat in gradually 1 cup of powdered sugar. When the mixture is fluffy, beat in 4 egg yolks one at a time. Then add 1 square (1 ounce) of unsweetened chocolate, first melted with 1 tablespoon of hot water, and 2 teaspoons of brandy. Blend the mixture well and fold in 4 stiffly beaten egg whites. Spoon the mousse into 4 individual glass dessert cups and chill it at least 8 hours or overnight. Serve with lady fingers.

This mousse can also be put in a mold lined first with waxed paper, then with split lady fingers. Cover the mousse with more lady fingers and serve it turned out on a chilled platter. Serves four.

THE JACKSON STREET FERRY   *New Orleans, Louisiana*

Shirred Eggs with Caper Sauce

(Eggs, butter, wine vinegar, capers)

To serve four, use 4 individual shirred-egg dishes and, on the top of the stove, melt 1 teaspoon of butter in each one. When the butter is hot, break 2 eggs into each dish, sprinkle the whites only with salt, and transfer the dishes to a preheated 350° oven. In a small saucepan melt 4 tablespoons of butter and let it bubble and brown but do not let it scorch. Take the pan off the fire, add 1 tablespoon of wine vinegar, stir well, add 1 tablespoon of capers, and return the pan to the heat for a few seconds. When the whites of the eggs are just set but the yolks are still soft, pour the caper sauce over them and serve immediately.

DOCKS AND SKYLINE   *Cleveland, Ohio*

SMOKED-SALMON OMELETTE

(Eggs, cream sauce, smoked salmon, capers)

In a small saucepan melt 1 tablespoon of butter, blend in 1 teaspoon of flour, and add gradually ½ cup of milk. Cook the sauce, stirring constantly, until it is smooth and thickened, and add ⅓ cup of minced Nova Scotia smoked salmon, ½ tablespoon of drained capers, and freshly ground pepper to taste. Keep this filling hot and make a 6-egg omelette as follows:

Put 1 tablespoon of butter in an omelette pan just hot enough to make the butter sizzle but not brown. Tilt the pan to coat the whole surface with butter, and when it stops sizzling, pour in the eggs, lightly beaten with 2 tablespoons of cold water. Stir them briskly with the flat of the fork, then let them set over medium heat, shaking the pan often. Lift the edge of the omelette to let the un-cooked egg on the surface run under, but do this as little as possible and still cook the omelette through. It should be soft and neither tough nor brown. When it is done, spread the salmon filling across the center and fold over one edge with a spatula. Slide the unfolded edge out of the pan onto a platter, then turn the pan completely over the platter. The omelette should land with the two edges neatly tucked under and the top golden and unbroken. Sprinkle with chopped parsley and serve immediately. Serves four.

CHURCH IN THE WHEAT LANDS
near Valley City, North Dakota

Standard Oil Company

Whole Wheat Bread

(Whole wheat flour, yeast, milk, brown sugar, salt, shortening)

Dissolve 2 cakes of yeast and 1 teaspoon of brown sugar in ½ cup of luke-warm water and let them stand for 10 minutes. Scald 2 cups of milk and pour it into a large bowl. In it dissolve ¼ cup of brown sugar and 1 tablespoon of salt, and let the milk cool to lukewarm. Stir in the dissolved yeast, then add 3 cups of whole wheat flour and 2 tablespoons of melted shortening. Beat the mixture thoroughly, then add gradually 3 to 3½ more cups of whole wheat flour, or enough to make a dough that does not stick to the hands. Turn the dough out onto a board lightly floured with white flour and knead it for 10 minutes until it is smooth. Then put it in a greased bowl, brush it with melted shortening, cover it with a cloth, and let it rise in a warm place until it is doubled in bulk, or for 1½ to 2 hours.

Put the dough back on the floured board, knead it quickly and thoroughly and divide it in half. Let it rest, covered, for 10 minutes, then shape each half to fit a standard bread pan. Grease 2 pans, put in the loaves and brush them with melted shortening. Cover them with a cloth and leave them in a warm place for 1 hour, or until the tops rise above the sides of the pans. Bake the loaves in a preheated 400° oven for 10 minutes, then lower the temperature to 375° and bake them another 40 minutes. Cool the loaves on wire racks.

22

RAINBOW ROW
Charleston, South Corolina

Samuel Chamberlain

Charleston Benne Biscuits

(Benné seeds, flour, shortening, cayenne pepper)

In a hot dry skillet brown lightly ¾ cup of benné (sesame) seed. Sift together into a bowl 2 cups of flour, ½ teaspoon of salt and a pinch of cayenne pepper. Mix in the browned benné seed, then cut in bit by bit ¾ cup of vegetable shortening. Work in about ¼ cup of ice water, or enough to give the mixture the consistency of pie crust dough. Roll the dough out a scant ¼ inch thick on a lightly floured board and cut it into tiny circles with a cookie cutter or a liqueur glass. Bake the benné biscuits on a cookie sheet in a 300° oven for 15 to 20 minutes. Sprinkle them with salt while they are hot. These biscuits should be stored in a covered jar and crisped in a slow oven just before serving.

23

MOUNT RAINIER *Rainier National Park, Washington*

ROAST PHEASANT

(Pheasant, onions, juniper berries, larding pork, chicken broth, marmalade)

Rub a cleaned 3- to 3½-pound pheasant inside and out with salt and pepper. Place 2 or 3 small whole onions, 2 or 3 juniper berries, and a lump of butter in the cavity. Truss the bird, rub a little butter on the legs, and tie a thin piece of larding pork over the breast. Put the pheasant in a small roasting pan, add ½ cup of clear chicken broth, and roast it in a preheated 350° over for 40 to 50 minutes, basting it often with the pan juices. After the first 15 minutes of roasting, turn the bird breast side down to brown the back, then turn it right side up again. Remove the larding pork 15 minutes before the pheasant is done to brown the breast. Put the bird on a hot platter and keep it warm. Skim the fat from the pan juices, dilute them with a little chicken broth and ¼ cup of dry white wine, add 2 level tablespoons of bitter-sweet English marmalade, and stir well. Simmer the sauce for 2 or 3 minutes, and pour it into a sauceboat. Garnish the platter with water cress. Serves three or four.

24

THE CLUB HOUSE　　　　　　　　　　　*Pine Mountain, Georgia*
Ida Cason Gardens

COUNTRY CAPTAIN

(Chicken, onions, green pepper, garlic, curry, herbs, tomatoes, currants, almonds)

Cut a 3-pound chicken into serving pieces and shake them in a paper bag with ¼ cup of flour, 1 teaspoon of salt, and ¼ teaspoon of pepper. In a large skillet sauté the chicken in 2 tablespoons each of hot butter and oil until it is well browned on all sides. Remove the chicken and keep it warm. In the fat remaining in the pan sauté 2 small minced onions until they are golden. Add a little butter if necessary. Add 1 minced green pepper and 1 minced and crushed clove of garlic, and simmer the vegetables together for 3 or 4 minutes. Then stir in 2 teaspoons of curry powder, or more to taste, 2 tablespoons of chopped parsley, a pinch of thyme, and 2 cups of Italian plum tomatoes. Simmer the sauce for 15 minutes, then return the chicken to the skillet and cook it, covered, for another 20 minutes, or until it is tender. Add ¼ cup of dried currants 5 minutes before the chicken is done. Serve Country Captain with fluffy white rice and sprinkled with blanched, split and toasted almonds. Serves four.

25

THE CLARA BARTON SCHOOLHOUSE (1851)   *Standard Oil Company*
Burlington, New Jersey

Open Blueberry Pie

(Pastry, blueberries, raspberry jelly)

Use your favorite rich pie pastry recipe. Line a pie plate with a thin layer of the pastry dough and chill it. Prick the pastry with a fork and bake the shell for 15 minutes in a 450° oven, or until it is lightly browned. Cool the shell and fill it with large fresh blueberries. Stir ¾ cup of raspberry jelly thoroughly with 2 tablespoons of water and spoon it over the blueberries. Heat the tart for 5 minutes in a hot oven just before serving. Serve it with a separate bowl of chilled whipped cream sweetened to taste.

PENNSYLVANIA DUTCH FARM   *Standard Oil Company*
near Allentown, Pennsylvania

German Sour Bean Salad

(Butter beans, onion, sour cream, vinegar, sugar, horseradish)

Cook 4 cups of butter beans (baby limas) in salted water to cover until they are just tender. Drain them and mix them with 1 medium onion, thinly sliced. Beat together with a fork 1 cup of sour cream, 1½ tablespoons of cider vinegar, 2 tablespoons of sugar, and horseradish and salt and pepper to taste. Add this dressing to the beans and let them marinate in it for at least 1 hour. Serve the bean salad cold and liberally sprinkled with chopped parsley. Serves six to eight.

LOCAL FISHERMAN   *Hatteras, North Carolina*

Baked Stuffed Rockfish (Striped Bass)

(Rockfish or striped bass, vegetables, herbs, bread crumbs, sherry, bacon, lemon)

Make a stuffing of 2 small onions, 1 stalk of celery with its leaves, and ½ green pepper, all minced and sautéed in 3 tablespoons of butter until soft, 1 cup of bread crumbs, 2 tablespoons of minced parsley, thyme, salt, pepper, and a little dry sherry to moisten. Stuff and sew up a 3- to 4-pound striped bass, place it in a small oiled roasting pan, cut 4 slits in the top side, and cover each slit with half a slice of bacon. Bake the fish in a 400° oven, allowing about 8 minutes per pound, basting occasionally with 3 tablespoons of butter and the juice of half a lemon mixed with ½ cup of boiling water. Serves six or more.

THE STATE CAPITOL   *Oklahoma City*

Southern Pecan Pie

(Pastry, butter, light brown sugar, eggs, cane syrup, vanilla, pecans)

Line a 9-inch pie plate with pastry. In a bowl cream together 4 tablespoons
of butter and 1 cup of firmly packed light brown sugar until the mixture is light
and fluffy. Add 4 beaten eggs, 1 cup of syrup (preferably Southern cane syrup,
but corn syrup will do), 1 teaspoon of vanilla, ¼ teaspoon of salt, and 1¼
cups of coarsely chopped pecan meats. Stir well, turn the mixture into the pastry
shell, and bake the pie in a preheated 450° oven for 10 minutes. Then lower the
heat to 350° and continue baking for 30 minutes, or until the filling is set. Serve
just barely warm; or serve chilled and covered with a layer of whipped cream
decorated with whole pecan halves. Serves six to eight.

CAPE COD WINDMILL   *Samuel Chamberlain*
Eastham, Massachusetts

JUNE PLATT'S CRANBERRY SAUCE DELUXE

(Cranberries, sugar, orange marmalade, lemon juice, almonds)

Blanch, peel and split ½ cup of almonds and soak them in ice water for 3 hours in the refrigerator. Meanwhile, wash and pick over 1 pound of cranberries. Put 2 cups of granulated sugar in a large saucepan, add 1 cup of water and bring the mixture to a boil without stirring it. Simmer the syrup for 5 minutes and add the cranberries; stir the mixture once thoroughly and cook it for about 3 minutes, or until the cranberries have all burst, but no longer than 5 minutes. Take the saucepan off the heat, add ½ cup of orange marmalade and the juice of 1½ lemons. When the cranberry sauce is cold, mix in the blanched almonds, thoroughly drained, and serve it well chilled. This makes about 3 pints.

FISHERMEN'S DOCK
Friendship, Maine

Samuel Chamberlain

Lobster Stew

(Lobster, butter, milk, cream, cayenne pepper)

Boil three 2-pound lobsters (in sea water if possible), crack the shells and remove the meat. Do this over a bowl so as to catch all the liquid that drains out. Reserve the green liver and any coral there may be, break up and save the shells, and cut the meat into small chunks.

In a large saucepan heat the lobster meat in 4 tablespoons of melted butter without letting it brown. Put the shells and the liquid that drained from them in another saucepan with 1 quart of milk. Bring this mixture slowly to a boil, simmer it for 5 minutes and pour it through a sieve over the lobster meat, discarding the shells. Mash the liver and the coral, mix them with ¾ cup of heavy cream and add them to the lobster stew. Bring the stew just to the boiling point, season it with a touch of cayenne pepper, and add salt if necessary and a lump of butter. Serve immediately in soup bowls with buttered and toasted chowder crackers. Serves six.

31

CRESCENT BEACH
Ecola State Park, Oregon

Union Pacific Railroad

Salmon Kedgeree

(Salmon, onions, butter, curry powder, parsley, hard-boiled eggs, rice)

This is a very old dish that was originally made in New England with codfish.
In the top of a double boiler, directly over the fire, cook 2 minced onions in 4 tablespoons of butter until they are soft. With a fork flake a 1-pound piece of poached salmon. To the onions add ¼ cup of the broth in which the fish was cooked (or ¼ cup of cream) and ½ teaspoon of curry powder. Blend the mixture thoroughly, then add the salmon and 2 tablespoons of chopped parsley. Simmer the fish over a low flame for 5 minutes, then add 2 cups of cooked rice, the chopped whites of 3 hard-boiled eggs, and salt and pepper to taste. Continue cooking the kedgeree over hot water until it is piping hot and add a little liquid if it seems dry. To serve it, pile it in a pyramid on a hot serving platter, sprinkle it with the sieved yolks of the 3 hard-boiled eggs and a little paprika, and surround the pyramid with broiled tomatoes. Serves four.

SPLIT-RAIL FENCE IN KENTUCKY   *Ewing Galloway*

PECAN BOURBON CANDIES

(Cocoa, powdered sugar, bourbon, corn syrup, vanilla wafers, pecans)

Sift together 2 tablespoons of dark unsweetened cocoa and 1 cup of powdered sugar. Stir in ¼ cup of bourbon mixed with 2 tablespoons of light corn syrup. Add 2½ cups of finely crushed vanilla wafers and 1 cup of coarsely chopped pecan meats. Blend the mixture thoroughly and roll it by hand into small balls. Dredge these lightly in another ½ cup of powdered sugar mixed with 2 teaspoons of cocoa. Store the bourbon balls in a cool place.

33

CENTRAL PARK New York City

Standard Oil Company

VICHYSSOISE DIAT

(Leeks, onion, butter, chicken stock, potatoes, milk, cream, chives)

This famous soup, though it is often thought of as a French specialty, was actually created in America at the old New York Ritz and is seldom found in Europe. The original recipe is the creation of the distinguished chef, Monsieur Louis Diat, who presided over the Ritz kitchens for more than forty years. It is printed here with his kind permission.

In a soup kettle sauté 1 medium onion and the white parts of 2 or 3 leeks, all finely sliced, in 1 tablespoon of melted butter until they are soft but not at all brown. Add 1 cup each of boiling water and hot chicken stock, 2 medium potatoes, quartered, and ½ teaspoon of salt. Simmer the soup for 30 minutes, or until the potatoes are soft, then force it through a fine sieve. Add 1 cup each of milk and light cream, bring the mixture back to a boil and strain it again. Cool the soup, stirring it occasionally; strain it a third time, through a very fine sieve, and stir in ½ cup of extra-heavy cream. Chill the Vichyssoise thoroughly and serve it with a sprinkling of finely chopped chives. Serves six.

GHOST TOWN FAÇADES
Virginia City, Nevada

Hubert A. Lowman

CHEESE CAKE

(Graham crackers, sugar, cinnamon, butter, eggs, cream cheese, lemon, sour cream)

Mix 1½ cups of fine graham cracker crumbs with 3 tablespoons of granulated sugar and ½ teaspoon of cinnamon. Melt 3 tablespoons of butter, blend it into the crumb mixture and press the crumbs firmly against the bottom and sides of a small spring-form cake pan or glass baking dish.

With a hand egg beater beat together 2 small eggs. Beat in 6 tablespoons of sugar and then bit by bit ¾ pound of cream cheese. Add ½ teaspoon of vanilla extract, the grated rind of half a lemon and ¼ teaspoon of lemon juice. Beat in 1½ cups of sour cream, and when the mixture is thoroughly blended fold in 2 tablespoons of melted butter with a spoon. Pour the batter into the lined cake pan and bake the cheese cake in a 350° oven for 30 minutes. While the cake is still hot it will not appear quite firm, but longer baking will make it dry. Cool the cake and chill it for 6 hours in the refrigerator to set before serving.

THE MAIN STREET *Ewing Galloway*
Harpers Ferry, West Virginia

Homemade Sausage Meat

(Lean and fat pork, herbs, spices)

Mix together thoroughly 1½ pounds of lean pork and ½ pound of fat pork, both ground, 2 teaspoons of salt, ½ tablespoon each of sage and orégano, 1 teaspoon of ground black pepper, ¼ teaspoon of cayenne pepper, 2 teaspoons of brown sugar, and 2 tablespoons of minced parsley. Pack the mixture in a crock or in any tightly covered container, and store it in the refrigerator overnight so that the meat can absorb the flavor of the spices. Raw pork should not be stored for long, so use the sausage meat the next day. Shape it into flat patties and brown them well on both sides in a skillet with a little butter. Serve the sausage patties with buttered hominy and fried apple rings. Serves four to six.

THE GOLDEN NUGGET
Las Vegas, Nevada

Union Pacific Railroad

Rock Salt Barbecue Steak

(Steak, rock salt, butter, Worcestershire, tarragon vinegar, garlic)

Wet several pounds of coarse rock salt with just enough water to make it stick together. Cover both sides and all the edges of a 4- to 5-pound sirloin steak with a layer of salt three quarters of an inch thick. Wrap the steak neatly in a double thickness of damp newspaper and put it on the outdoor grill over a bed of fiercely glowing coals. The paper will burn off, of course, and the salt will glaze into a hard crust. Turn the steak several times to cook it evenly. With a really good fire going, 18 to 25 minutes should be enough time for a rare or a medium-rare steak.

Take the steak off the grill with fire tongs and break off the salt shell with a hammer. Slice the steak in a shallow roasting pan in which plenty of butter has been melted to serve as a sauce. This can take up to a pound and the butter should be liberally seasoned with Worcestershire, tarragon vinegar, crushed garlic, and salt and pepper. Bring the seasoned butter to the sizzling point, stirring briskly, just before the steak is to be sliced. The juice from the steak is the finishing touch to the sauce. Serves eight to ten.

37

FIRST CONGREGATIONAL MEETING HOUSE (1824) *Samuel Chamberlain*
Stockbridge, Massachusetts

IRIS MOREY'S WEDDING CAKE

(This is the proper kind of wedding cake, an old-fashioned, 12-egg fruit cake)

In a large bowl cream together 2 cups of butter and 2 packed cups of brown sugar. Then mix in thoroughly, one by one, the following: 1 cup of molasses; 12 well-beaten egg yolks; 3½ cups of flour sifted with 4 teaspoons each of cinnamon and allspice and 1 teaspoon each of mace and nutmeg; 2 pounds of chopped mixed candied fruits, 3 pounds of chopped and seeded sultana raisins, 2 pounds of seedless raisins and 1 pound of currants — all these fruits first mixed and dredged together with ¾ cup of flour; 1 cup of grape juice; 1 pint of strawberry jam; 4 squares of chocolate, melted; 12 stiffly-beaten egg whites; and finally, ½ teaspoon of soda dissolved in a little hot water.

Butter a large round cake tin and line the bottom with 3 layers of brown paper cut to fit. Butter the top layer, pour in the batter (the tin should be about three-quarters full) and cover it with another buttered circle of paper. Set the tin in a pan of water and steam the cake for 3 hours in a 300° oven; then remove the pan of water and bake the cake 3 more hours. Turn it out on a rack to cool; then pour over it ½ cup or more of brandy.

This cake may be eaten right away. The original recipe, however, calls for it to mellow in a cool place, in an airtight container, for 6 weeks.

GRAIN ELEVATORS AT SUNSET
Kolin, Montana

Cities Service Company

CORN OYSTERS

(Corn, eggs, cracker crumbs, baking powder)

Mix 2 cups of raw corn, freshly grated from the cob, with 2 well-beaten eggs, ½ cup of fine cracker crumbs mixed with ¼ teaspoon of baking powder, and salt and pepper to taste. Drop the batter by small spoonfuls onto a hot, well-buttered griddle, and fry them quickly, turning them once, until they are golden brown on both sides. Serves four to six.

VILLAGE LANE   *Samuel Chamberlain*
Newcastle, Delaware

MUSHROOM AND SHAD ROE HORS-D'OEUVRE

(Mushrooms, shad roe, butter, onion, lemon juice, cream, brandy)

For 2 dozen small fresh mushrooms poach 1 shad roe (6 to 8 ounces) with several slices of lemon in water to cover for 15 minutes. Drain the roe, remove the outside membranes, and mash it with 2 tablespoons of soft butter, 1 small onion, grated, the juice of half a lemon, 2 tablespoons of heavy cream, 1 table-spoon of brandy, and salt and pepper to taste. Remove the stems from the mushrooms and stuff the caps with the seasoned roe. Arrange them on a buttered ovenproof serving dish and bake them in a 400° oven for 15 minutes. Spear each one with a toothpick and pass them immediately for a hot cocktail hors-d'oeuvre.

40

LAKE YELLOWSTONE   *Northern Pacific Railway*
Yellowstone National Park, Wyoming

ROAST WILD DUCK

(Wild duck, salt pork, stock, lime juice, currant jelly)

Hang wild ducks 48 hours to a week, depending on the temperature and on how gamey you want them to be. Pluck them dry and draw them no more than 3 hours before they are to be roasted. Remove the oil glands on either side of the tails and clip the wing tips. Wipe the ducks inside and out with a damp cloth and season them inside and out with salt and pepper. Wild ducks should *never* be washed.

Put a few cranberries or a quartered apple in each cavity and cover the breasts with thin slices of salt pork or bacon. Place the ducks in a shallow roasting pan and add a little water or red wine to the pan. Put them in a preheated 500° oven and roast them for 15 minutes, or very rare for knowledgeable hunters, 20 minutes for a medium-rare compromise. Baste the ducks every 5 minutes with the pan juices. Serve the ducks immediately, with wild rice. In a sauceboat serve the pan juices, well-skimmed and diluted with ½ to ¾ cup of stock or consommé, the juice of ½ a lime and 2 tablespoons of currant jelly. Add salt and pepper to taste. Two 2½-pound wild ducks serve four.

MOUNT ST. HELENS
Spirit Lake, Washington

Northern Pacific Railway

Baked Salmon Trout

(Salmon trout, bacon, lemon, lettuce, onion, butter)

Clean, trim and wipe dry a handsome salmon trout. Remove the head and tail or not, as you wish. Rub the fish inside and out with salt and pepper and stuff it with 1 or 2 slices of bacon and a few slices of lemon. Lay it in a large baking dish on a good bed of lettuce leaves, spread it with thin slices of onion and a few slices of lemon and dot it generously with butter. Put the trout in a very hot, preheated oven, but reduce the heat immediately to 350°. Bake it for 30 minutes or more, depending on the size of the trout, or until the meat flakes easily at the touch of a fork. Baste the trout every 5 minutes with the liquid given off by the lettuce leaves, and discard the lettuce before serving.

If the trout is a large one, it is best to use a baking dish that can be brought to the table, as it will be difficult to move the whole fish to a platter without breaking it.

42

THE WREN BUILDING
College of William and Mary, Williamsburg, Virginia

Samuel Chamberlain

BATTER BREAD

(White water-ground corn meal, salt, butter, eggs, milk, baking powder)

Scald 2 cups of white water-ground corn meal with 1 cup of boiling water, or just enough to wet it without making it soft. Let the mixture stand for 2 or 3 minutes, then add 1 teaspoon of salt and another ½ cup of boiling water, or just enough to give it the consistency of a soft dough. Mix in 1½ tablespoons of melted butter and let the corn meal cool. Then beat in 4 large eggs, well-beaten, 2 cups of milk, and finally, 1 teaspoon of baking powder. Pour the batter into a deep baking dish, well-buttered, and bake it in a 350° oven for about 1 hour, or until the batter bread is puffed and brown on top and crusty brown on the bottom (the best part of it!) Serves six.

43

THE COLUMBIA RIVER GORGE   *Oregon*
from Crown Point

Broiled Sirloin with Blue Cheese

(Sirloin steak, blue cheese, cream, mushrooms, onion)

Mash together to a paste ⅓ pound of blue cheese, 2 tablespoons of heavy cream, ½ cup of minced fresh mushrooms sautéed in a little butter until they are soft, 1 tablespoon of finely minced white onion, a dash of Worcestershire, and a little freshly ground pepper. Use a sirloin steak weighing 2½ to 3 pounds and cut at least 2 inches thick. Preheat the broiler, and broil the steak 2 inches from the heat for 6 to 7 minutes. Turn it and broil it on the other side for 5 minutes. Then spread the blue-cheese mixture on it and put it back under the flame for 2 minutes. The timing is actually a matter of practice, but with a really hot broiler these directions should give you a medium-rare steak with the cheese melted to a rich creamy sauce. Serves four to six.

44

SNOW SCENE   *Ipswich, Massachusetts*

Pork Chops with Apples

(Loin pork chops, rosemary, butter, apples, cider)

Trim the fat from 6 thick loin pork chops and season them lightly with a mixture of salt, freshly ground pepper and powdered rosemary. In a skillet brown the chops well on both sides in 1 tablespoon of butter. Place them in one layer in a shallow baking dish and cover them with 3 tart apples, peeled, cored and sliced. Add ½ cup of hot water to the juices left in the skillet, stir well, pour this into the casserole, and add ¾ cup of cider. Sprinkle the apples with a little salt and 2 tablespoons of brown sugar, and dot them with butter. Bake the chops, covered, in a 300° oven, basting occasionally, for 45 minutes to 1 hour, or until they are well done and the sauce is reduced. Serves six.

45

YACHT BASIN IN MIAMI, FLORIDA   *Cities Service Company*

LEMON SPONGE

(Gelatin, lemon, eggs, sugar, whipped cream, macaroons)

Soak 1 tablespoon of gelatin in 2 tablespoons of water; add 6 tablespoons of lemon juice and set the mixture over hot water to dissolve the gelatin. Beat 3 egg yolks in a bowl until they are light, and add ⅓ cup of sugar and the lemon-gelatin mixture. In another bowl beat 3 egg whites until they are stiff, adding gradually another ⅓ cup of sugar and the grated zest of 1½ lemons. Fold the egg-white mixture carefully into the yolk mixture, turn the lemon sponge into a glass serving bowl and chill it thoroughly. Dry out several macaroons in a slow oven and crumble them finely. Just before serving the lemon sponge, spread it with whipped cream and sprinkle the cream with the macaroon crumbs. Serves four.

46

AUTUMN AT CHENOA, ILLINOIS

BOILED BEEF AND CREAM HORSERADISH SAUCE

(Bottom round of beef, vinegar, vegetables, herbs, spices, cream, horseradish)

Rub a 4-pound piece of bottom round with salt and pepper and put it in an earthenware bowl. Add 2 cups of water, 2 cups of cider vinegar, 2 onions and 1 carrot, all sliced, 2 cut cloves of garlic, a handful of celery leaves, 2 bay leaves, a pinch of thyme, a dozen peppercorns and 4 whole cloves. Marinate the beef, tightly covered, in the refrigerator for 2, 3 or even 4 days, turning it at least twice a day.

Remove the beef and brown it well on both sides in a skillet in 1 tablespoon of melted fat. Then put 2 cups of the marinade, the vegetables and the meat all in a heavy covered pot and simmer them over a low flame for about 3½ hours, or until the meat is very tender. Add more marinade during the cooking if extra liquid is needed. Carve the beef in thick slices on a hot platter, strain some of the juice from the pot over it and sprinkle it with chopped parsley. Serve it with boiled potatoes and this fluffy horseradish sauce:

Whip ½ cup of heavy cream until it is stiff and combine it with 4 to 6 tablespoons of prepared horseradish, well-drained, ½ teaspoon of dry mustard, 1 teaspoon of sugar, and salt and pepper to taste.

47

STANTON HALL　　　　　　　　　　　　　　　　*Natchez, Mississippi*

Sweet Potato Croquettes

(Sweet potatoes, eggs, butter, nutmeg, pecans)

Boil, peel and mash enough sweet potatoes to make 2 cups. Add 1 beaten egg, 3 tablespoons of melted butter, and salt, pepper and freshly grated nutmeg to taste. Beat well with a wooden spoon and add a little hot milk if the mixture is too dry. Form it into 8 balls, dip them in an egg beaten with 1 tablespoon of water, and roll them in finely ground pecan meats or bread crumbs. Fry the croquettes in deep hot fat (390°) until they are golden brown, and drain them on brown paper. You *can* put a marshmallow in the center of each croquette if you like that sort of thing. Serves four.

THE GOLDEN GATE BRIDGE   *San Francisco, California*

CHINESE ALMOND CAKES

(Flour, sugar, baking powder, shortening, egg, almond extract, almonds)

Sift together 2½ cups of flour, 1 cup of fine granulated sugar, 1 teaspoon of baking powder, and ¼ teaspoon of salt. With a knife cut in 1 cup of shortening, preferably lard, and add 1 egg and 1 teaspoon of almond extract. Mix well with a fork and add 1 to 2 tablespoons of water if the dough is very stiff. Knead the dough until it is smooth and chill it for 1 hour. Form it into balls the size of a large walnut and press them down with the palm of the hand to make cakes not quite ½ inch thick. Press a blanched almond into the center of each one and bake the cakes, set well apart on a floured baking sheet, in a 400° oven for 5 minutes; then lower the heat to 325° and bake them for another 10 minutes, or until they are an even golden color but not yet brown. Makes about 3 dozen.

49

MISION SAN DIEGO DEL ALCALÁ   *Union Pacific Railroad*
near San Diego, California

CAESAR SALAD

(Romaine, olive oil, garlic, egg, lemon, anchovies, Parmesan, French bread)

Wash a large head of romaine and shake the water from it very thoroughly. Sauté 1 cup of diced stale French bread in 2 tablespoons of hot olive oil, flavored with a touch of garlic, until the croutons are golden brown on all sides, and drain them on brown paper. Boil 1 egg for 1 minute.

Break the romaine into a wooden salad bowl that has been rubbed with a cut clove of garlic. Sprinkle the greens with ¼ teaspoon of salt and plenty of freshly ground black pepper, and add 4 tablespoons of olive oil flavored with ½ clove of crushed garlic. Toss the salad thoroughly, then break in the 1-minute egg, squeeze in the juice of ½ a large lemon, add 4 anchovies, cut in small pieces, and toss the salad again. Taste for seasoning and add lemon juice and salt if they are needed. Then add ¼ cup of grated Parmesan cheese and the croutons, toss the Caesar salad once more and serve it immediately, with a loaf of hot French bread. Serves four to six.

MOUNT VERNON, VIRGINIA   *Samuel Chamberlain*

QUICK SALLY LUNN

(Shortening, sugar, eggs, flour, baking powder, salt, milk)

Cream together ½ cup of shortening and ½ cup of sugar. Add 3 eggs and beat the mixture well. Measure 2 cups of sifted flour and resift it with 2 teaspoons of baking powder and ¾ teaspoon of salt. Add the sifted mixture to the batter in 3 parts alternately with 1 cup of milk. Beat the batter lightly just long enough to blend it smoothly. Bake the Sally Lunn in a 425° oven for 30 minutes in a buttered funnel cake pan, or for 15 minutes in muffin pans. Serve immediately, piping hot, with butter, for tea.

51

AMERICAN-GOTHIC CHURCH   *Beverly, West Virginia*

GOLDENROD STUFFED EGGS

(Hard-boiled eggs, mayonnaise, lemon juice, mustard, chives, French peas)

Cut hard-boiled eggs in half lengthwise, remove the yolks, and reserve half of them. Mash the rest with enough mayonnaise, and with lemon juice and prepared mustard to taste, to make a smooth, fairly thin purée. Add salt, freshly ground pepper and plenty of minced fresh chives. Then add tiny French peas, well-drained, using approximately equal amounts of peas and egg purée. Chill this mixture and stuff the whites generously with it shortly before serving. Force some of the reserved yolks through a sieve, sprinkle them over the stuffed eggs, and decorate each egg with a small sprig of parsley.

UPSTATE FARMYARD　　　　　　　　　　　　*near Lowville, New York*

Strawberry Mousse

(Strawberries, whipped cream, egg white, sugar, vanilla)

This is a recipe to entertain children in the winter, and delicious at any time of the year. Use fresh or frozen strawberries, according to the season.

Crush 1 quart of fresh strawberries, or thaw and crush 1 package of frozen strawberries. Whip 1 pint of heavy cream and beat 1 egg white stiff. Fold together lightly the cream, egg white and strawberries, and add fine granulated sugar to taste and ½ teaspoon of vanilla. Put the mousse in a metal canister with a tightly-fitting lid and tie a folded dish towel firmly around the edge of the lid. Dig a hole in a snowbank and line it with rock salt. Put the canister in the hole, pack it down firmly with snow, and leave it to freeze for several hours. Lacking a snowbank, freeze the mousse, covered with waxed paper, in a deep refrigerator tray for 3 hours with the controls set at "very cold." Serves six.

COVERED BRIDGE
Jackson, New Hampshire

Samuel Chamberlain

Indian Pudding

(Milk, yellow corn meal, molasses, sugar, butter, cinnamon, nutmeg or ginger)

In the top of a double boiler scald 3 cups of milk. Mix 4 level tablespoons of yellow corn meal with ¼ cup of milk and stir it into the hot milk. Cook the mixture for 15 minutes over hot water, then add ⅔ cup of dark molasses, ⅓ cup of sugar, and 4 tablespoons of butter. Season the batter with ¾ teaspoon of cinnamon and ⅜ teaspoon of either grated nutmeg or powdered ginger. Cook the batter for another 5 minutes, then turn it into a well-buttered baking dish. Pour on ¾ cup of cold milk (under no circumstances must the milk be stirred in) and bake the Indan pudding in a 300° oven for 3 hours. Then let it stand to set for 30 minutes and serve it warm, with a hard sauce flavored with rum.

THE FOUNTAINS IN LOGAN CIRCLE   *A. Devaney*
Philadelphia, Pennsylvania

PHILADELPHIA PEACH ICE CREAM

(Peaches, sugar, lemon juice, light cream)

Mix 2 cups of ripe, peeled and chopped peaches with 1 cup of granulated sugar and let them stand for 30 minutes. Force the mixture through a colander, add ½ teaspoon of lemon juice and stir in 2 cups of light cream.

This ice cream should of course be made in a hand freezer. However, if it *must* be done in the refrigerator, turn the controls to "very cold" and put the cream in a deep ice tray in the freezing compartment until it reaches the mushy stage. Then spoon it into a chilled bowl and beat it hard with an egg beater. Return it to the tray, freeze it some more, beat it again, then leave it to freeze solid for at least 3 hours, covered with wax paper to keep crystals from forming on top. Serves six.

MACKINAC ISLAND, MICHIGAN   *Ewing Galloway*

Scalloped Eggs and Onions

(Eggs, onions, bacon, white sauce, nutmeg, bread crumbs)

Hard-boil 4 eggs, peel and slice 6 small white onions, and fry 6 slices of bacon until they are crisp. In a saucepan blend 3 tablespoons of flour into 3 tablespoons of melted butter, add gradually 1½ cups of milk and ½ cup of cream. Stir this white sauce constantly until it is medium-thick and season it with a pinch of grated nutmeg and salt and pepper to taste.

Cover the bottom of a well-buttered baking dish with one third of the white sauce and over it spread one third of the sliced onions. Crumble 3 of the slices of bacon over the onions, then arrange 2 of the hard-boiled eggs, sliced, over the bacon. Repeat these layers, starting with half of the remaining white sauce and half the remaining onions. Then add one more layer of onions and the rest of the sauce. Sprinkle the top with fine bread crumbs, dot with butter and bake the scalloped eggs in a 350° oven for 1¼ hours. Serves four.

THE UNITED NATIONS FROM THE EAST RIVER *United Nations*
New York City

International Lamb Curry

(Lamb, onion, garlic, celery, apple, ginger, chili, curry, chicken stock, raisins)

East Indian curry, or a homegrown version of it, has become an American favorite for cooks and hostesses planning a special-occasion menu:

In a heavy casserole sauté 1 chopped onion and 1 crushed clove of garlic in 4 tablespoons of butter until they are golden. Add 2 stalks of celery and one small green apple, all chopped, 3 tablespoons of minced candied ginger, and ½ teaspoon of chili powder. Cook the mixture until all the vegetables are soft, then blend in 2 teaspoons of tomato paste, 1 tablespoon of flour and 1½ tablespoon of curry powder. (This amount of curry makes a fairly mild sauce; add curry and chili cautiously to taste for a hotter one.) Stir in slowly 3 cups of chicken stock or consommé and add ½ cup of seedless raisins, 3 cups of diced cooked lamb and salt to taste. Simmer the curry, covered, over a low flame for 45 minutes, until the sauce is somewhat reduced. Serve with boiled rice, Major Grey's chutney and saucers of condiments such as minced green pepper, minced raw onion seasoned with olive oil and black pepper, grated fresh coconut, chopped hard-boiled egg, crumbled bacon and chopped candied ginger. Serves four.

INDIAN PUEBLO
Taos, New Mexico

Sante Fe Railway

Chilis Rellenos

(Green chili peppers, cheese, eggs, onion, garlic, tomatoes, chili powder, herbs)

Put green chili peppers (or regular green peppers) under a hot broiler flame for 10 to 15 minutes, turning them often to blister the skins on all sides. Wrap the peppers in a dish towel, let them cool, and scrape off the thin skins. If the peppers are large, cut them in half lengthwise; if they are small chilis, slit them down one side. Remove the cores and all the seeds and membranes.

Stuff the peppers with a stick of Monterey Jack or mozzarella cheese and close them around the cheese with a wooden toothpick. For 8 small chilis, combine 2 beaten egg yolks, ¼ teaspoon of salt and 1½ tablespoons of flour, and fold in 2 stiffly beaten egg whites. Drop the chilis in this batter, ladle them out with a big spoon and drop them into hot fat ½ inch deep in a skillet. Turn them twice and drain them on brown paper when they are golden brown on all sides.

Fifteen minutes before servingtime, reheat the chilis in a Mexican sauce made by simmering together for 35 minutes 2 tablespoons of bacon fat, 1 small onion and 2 cloves of garlic, all minced, 2½ cups of Italian plum tomatoes, 2 teaspoons of chili powder (or more to taste), 1 tablespoon of minced parsley, a pinch each of thyme and sage, and salt and pepper. Serves four to six.

58

APPROACH TO MANHATTAN
New York City

Cities Service Company

Steak Barry Wall

(Steak, butter, dry mustard, Worcestershire, parsley)

For a 2-pound, 1½-inch steak, blend 2 teaspoons of butter with ½ teaspoon of dry English mustard, 1 teaspoon of Worcestershire and 1 teaspoon of minced parsley. Broil the steak under a hot flame for 3 to 4 minutes on each side. Then with a sharp knife crisscross 5 or 6 diagonal slashes on one side of the steak. Spread on the seasoned butter, sprinkle the steak with salt and plenty of freshly-ground black pepper, and broil it for 1 more minute. Serves four.

BRIDGE OVER THE MISSISSIPPI
Minneapolis, Minnesota

Ewing Galloway

BAKED WILD RICE AND TURKEY

(Wild rice, turkey, mushrooms, stock, cream, grated cheese)

Wash 1 cup of wild rice thoroughly and soak it in water to cover for 2 hours (or follow the instructions on the box for washing the rice). Drain it and in a bowl mix it with 2 cups of cooked turkey, cut in large dice, and ½ pound of mushrooms, sliced and sautéed briefly in 3 tablespoons of butter. Add 1½ cups each of turkey stock and cream and season with a little grated nutmeg and salt and pepper. Transfer the mixture to a generously buttered casserole and bake it, covered, in a 350° oven for 1 hour. Then add another cup of stock and bake the casserole for another 30 minutes, or until the rice is tender. Sprinkle the top with grated cheese, dot it with butter and brown it under the broiler flame just before serving. Serves four.

SUNSET OVER KANSAS CITY, MISSOURI   *Hubert A. Lowman*

FRESH MINT JELLY

(Fresh mint, tart apples, sugar)

Wash and slice enough tart apples to make 2 quarts of fruit; do not core or peel them, but do remove the stems and blossom ends. Bring 1 quart of water to a boil, add the apples and simmer them until they are soft. Tie 4 layers of cheese cloth over the top of a large kettle, laddle the cooked apples and their juice into the cheese cloth and let the juice drip through, without disturbing the apple pulp, for at least 6 hours.

Pour 1 cup of boiling water over 1 cup of firmly packed fresh mint leaves and let them steep for 1 hour; then press as much juice as possible from them and strain it. Measure the drained apple juice and for each cup add 2 tablespoons of the fresh mint extract. Bring the juice to a rolling boil and for each cup stir in ¾ cup of sugar and keep stirring until it is thoroughly dissolved. Boil the syrup rapidly until it sheets from the spoon, or until it reaches about 220° on a candy thermometer. Add a few drops of green food coloring and pour the syrup into hot jelly glasses. Seal them with paraffin when the jelly has set.

61

THE STARTING LINE   *Samuel Chamberlain*
Marblehead, Massachusetts

SPITE HOUSE FISH CHOWDER

(Haddock fillets, salt pork, onions, potatoes, milk)

Try out ¾ pound of finely diced salt pork in a skillet until the pieces are golden brown and drain them thoroughly on brown paper. Then brown lightly 6 large onions, sliced, in the fat left in the skillet. Meanwhile, in a soup kettle boil 6 small potatoes, peeled and diced, for 10 minutes in just enough water to cover. Cut 2 pounds of haddock fillets into 1-inch pieces and add them to the kettle. With a slotted spoon remove the brown onions from the skillet, draining off as much fat as possible, and spread them over the fish. Discard all but 1 tablespoon of the fat. Into this blend 2 tablespoons of flour, stir in slowly 1 quart of milk, and add a dash of Worcestershire and salt and pepper to taste. Pour the seasoned milk into the kettle and simmer the chowder, covered, over the lowest possible flame for 3 hours without stirring it. Twenty minutes before servingtime, stir the chowder thoroughly and heat the browned salt pork in a slow oven until it is crisp. Taste the chowder for seasoning and serve it in soup bowls with buttered and toasted chowder crackers and a sprinkling of the crisp pork scraps. Serves six to eight.

BLESSING OF THE SHRIMP FLEET
Barataria, Louisiana

Standard Oil Company

SHRIMP CREOLE

(Shrimp, onions, garlic, sweet pepper, celery, herbs, spices, tomatoes)

Poach 2 pounds of raw shrimp for 8 minutes in boiling water to cover, drain them, and reserve the liquid. Shell and devein the shrimp.

In a skillet sauté 3 small onions, finely chopped, in 2 tablespoons of bacon fat until they are soft. Add 2 minced cloves of garlic and ½ a large sweet pepper, finely chopped, and cook the vegetables over a very low flame for 5 more minutes. Then add 1 small stalk of celery, finely chopped, 2 tablespoons of minced parsley, a good pinch of thyme, 2 bay leaves, 3 whole allspice, 1 tablespoon of Worcestershire, a dash of Tabasco, 1 teaspoon of sugar, 1 teaspoon of salt and a generous grinding of black pepper. Stir the mixture briskly and blend in 1½ tablespoons of flour. Add ½ cup of the shrimp liquor and 2½ cups of Italian plum tomatoes, and simmer the Creole sauce, covered, for 25 minutes. Then add the shrimp and more shrimp liquor if the sauce has reduced too quickly, and simmer them together for 15 minutes. Serve with buttered boiled rice. Serves four to six.

THE HOME OF PRESIDENT JAMES POLK   *Ewing Galloway*
Columbia, Tennessee

Minced Veal in Cream

(Cooked veal, scallions, milk, cream, egg, celery, parsley, mace, lemon)

In a skillet sauté the white parts of 2 scallions, chopped, in 2 tablespoons of butter until they are soft but not brown. Blend in 1½ tablespoons of flour and add slowly 1 cup each of milk and cream. Let the sauce thicken slightly and add the mashed yolk and finely chopped white of 1 hard-boiled egg and 1 tablespoon each of finely chopped celery and parsley. Add 2 cups of minced cooked veal and season with salt, white pepper and a pinch of mace. Heat the creamed veal just to the boiling point and serve it over boiled rice, garnished with chopped parsley and paper-thin quartered slices of lemon. Serves four.

THE OPERA HOUSE
Sun Valley, Idaho

Union Pacific Railroad

CHRISTMAS WREATH COOKIES

(Butter, sugar, orange rind, egg, flour, green sugar, cinnamon candies)

Cream together ¾ cup of butter and ½ cup of sugar and add 1 teaspoon of grated orange rind and 1 beaten egg. Beat the mixture with a spoon until it is light, then add 2 cups of sifted flour and stir the batter until it is thoroughly blended. Chill it for at least 1 hour, or until it is firm enough to roll.

Roll the dough out one eighth of an inch thick on a lightly floured board and cut it into circles with a 2-inch floured doughnut cutter. Arrange the circles on a greased baking sheet and brush them with a light meringue made of 1 egg white beaten stiff with 2 tablespoons of sugar. Sprinkle the cookies with green sugar and decorate them with red cinnamon candies clustered together like holly berries. Bake the wreaths in a 400° oven for 10 to 12 minutes and cool them on wire racks. (To make the green sugar, rub a few drops of food coloring into ½ cup of granulated sugar and put it in a slow oven, with the door open, to dry.) Makes about 4 dozen cookies.

RANCH NEAR EL PASO, TEXAS   *American Airlines*

Eggs in Hell

(Eggs, onions, green pepper, garlic, herbs, spices, meat extract, tomatoes)

In a skillet sauté slowly 2 small onions, thinly sliced, in 2 tablespoons of butter for 5 minutes. Add ½ a large green pepper, chopped, 1 minced clove of garlic, 1 tablespoon of chopped parsley, a pinch of thyme, ¼ teaspoon of dry mustard and a dash of Worcestershire. Simmer all together for another 5 minutes, stirring often. Add ¼ teaspoon of meat extract, 2½ cups of Italian plum tomatoes, 1 bay leaf, ½ teaspoon of sugar, a few grains of cayenne pepper, ½ teaspoon of chili powder, and salt and pepper to taste. Simmer the sauce, covered, over a low flame for 40 minutes.

Divide the sauce between 4 ovenproof onion soup bowls. Break 1 or 2 eggs into each bowl, sprinkle them with a little grated cheese, dot each one with butter and bake them in a 350° oven for 15 minutes, or until the whites are set. Serve with toasted and buttered French bread. Serves four.

SAN XAVIER DEL BAC
Tucson, Arizona

American Airlines

GUACAMOLE

(Avocado, lemon juice, onion, salt, chili powder)

Choose very ripe avocados. For each one start with 1 teaspoon of lemon juice, 2 teaspoons of grated onion, ¼ teaspoon of salt and ¼ teaspoon of chili powder. Mash the avocado pulp to a smooth paste in a bowl that has been rubbed with a cut clove of garlic, add the seasonings and taste. The Mexicans like their guacamole burning hot; keep adding salt and chili to yours until it is as spicy as you want it. Cover the guacamole with a very thin layer of mayonnaise to keep it from darkening, and mix it in thoroughly just before serving. Guacamole is an ideal cocktail dip for crisp raw vegetables. For a salad, pile the guacamole generously on thick slices of ripe, red tomatoes, arrange them on a platter and sprinkle them with crumbled bacon.

COUNTRY CHURCH   *Brooklyn, Connecticut*

RASPBERRIES AND WHIPPED CREAM CHEESE

(Raspberries, cream cheese, heavy cream, sugar, mint)

Cream together 12 ounces of cream cheese and ½ cup of heavy cream. Add ⅛ teaspoon of salt and beat the mixture until it is soft and smooth. Whip ¾ cup of heavy cream and mix it into the beaten cream cheese. Arrange the cheese in a smooth mound in the center of a platter and chill it until it is firm.

In an electric blender purée 3 cups of fresh raspberries, strain out the seeds through a fine sieve, and sweeten the sauce to taste. Just before serving, surround the cheese with more fresh raspberries, dust them and the cheese lightly with sugar, and decorate the platter with a few sprigs of fresh mint. Serve the sauce separately. Serves six.

CHERRY BLOSSOMS AND THE JEFFERSON MEMORIAL   *Washington, D.C.*

Filbert Pudding

(Filberts, gelatin, egg yolks, sugar, milk, cream, brandy, butter, apricots)

Soak 1 envelope of gelatin in 2 tablespoons of cold milk. In the top of a double boiler beat together ½ cup of sugar and 2 egg yolks until the mixture is light. Scald 2 cups of milk, stir in the gelatin, and add this to the yolk-sugar mixture gradually, stirring constantly. Stir the custard over barely simmering water until it thickens, and let it cool. Grind coarsely enough filberts (or walnuts, or pecans) to make ½ cup, and whip 1 cup of heavy cream. Stir the nuts into the cooled custard, add 2 tablespoons of brandy, and fold in the whipped cream. Pour the pudding into a glass serving dish and chill it until it is set. Serve it with a hot apricot sauce: In an electric blender purée 1½ cups of stewed apricots; strain the purée, heat it with 1 tablespoon of butter just to the boiling point, and add 1 tablespoon of brandy. Serves six.

69

MEDWAY PLANTATION
near Charleston, South Carolina

Samuel Chamberlain

Sweet Potato Souffle

(Sweet potatoes, milk, sherry, butter, spices, eggs)

In a bowl beat together 2 cups of hot mashed sweet potatoes, ½ cup of hot milk, 6 tablespoons of butter and ¼ cup of sherry. Season the potatoes with a pinch each of cayenne pepper and grated nutmeg, 1 teaspoon of grated lemon rind and ½ teaspoon of salt. When the mixture is smoothly blended, beat in 4 well-beaten egg yolks, then fold in 4 stiffly beaten egg whites. Transfer the batter to a buttered soufflé mold, bake it in a 400° oven for 25 minutes, or until the soufflé is nicely puffed and just beginning to brown, and serve it immediately. Serves four to six.

IN THE FRENCH QUARTER
New Orleans, Louisiana

Cities Service Company

Corn Bread and Pecan Stuffing for Turkey

(Turkey liver, onions, butter, corn bread, celery, parsley, thyme, stock, pecans)

Sauté the raw turkey liver and 3 medium onions, all chopped, in 6 tablespoons of melted butter for 3 or 4 minutes. In a bowl mix the liver and onions with 4 cups of crumbled corn bread (the center only, not the crust), 1 cup of chopped celery, ½ cup of chopped parsley and 1 teaspoon of dried thyme. Moisten the stuffing with turkey stock or consommé and with a fork mix in 2 cups of broken pecan meats. Season the stuffing with 1½ teaspoons of salt and a generous grinding of black pepper. This is enough dressing to stuff loosely a 10- to 12-pound Thanksgiving turkey.

71

THE CHICAGO RIVER   *Chicago, Illinois*

BEEF STROGANOFF

(Beef tenderloin, butter, beef broth, ginger, mushrooms, onion, sour cream)

Order 2 pounds of beef tenderloin cut in slices ¼ inch thick. Cut the slices into finger-size strips and sprinkle them lightly with salt and freshly ground pepper. In a saucepan blend 1 tablespoon of flour into 2 tablespoons of melted butter and add gradually 1 cup of hot beef broth. Season the sauce with a little powdered ginger and simmer it, stirring often, until it thickens. Meanwhile, in a skillet sauté ¼ pound of sliced mushrooms in 2 tablespoons of butter. In a second skillet sauté 1 small onion, minced, in 2 tablespoons of butter until it is golden. Add the seasoned beef to the onion and cook it quickly, turning the pieces often so they will brown evenly, for 5 or 6 minutes. It should be brown but a little pink in the center. Add the mushrooms and the beef to the simmering sauce, and stir in gradually 1½ cups of sour cream. Continue cooking only just long enough to heat the cream, stirring constantly. Taste for seasoning and serve with rice or kasha (see *Index*). Serves six.

SPORT FISHING BOATS AT DEPOE BAY   *Oregon*

Broiled King Crab Legs

(King crab legs, lemon juice, butter, pepper)

Huge Alaska King crab legs are a specialty of the west coast, but they are now shipped, usually boiled and frozen, to markets all over the country. Two King crab legs will serve three. Break them into sections, slit the roundest side of the shells lengthwise with scissors, snip them crosswise in several places along the slit and pull it open about an inch. Pour a spoonful of sauce made of 1 part lemon juice and 2 parts melted butter over the meat, grind a little pepper over it, and broil the crab legs, not too close to the flame, for about 10 minutes, or just long enough to brown the shells. Baste the meat 3 or 4 times with the lemon-butter sauce and serve it in the shells with a bowl of extra sauce, steamed wild rice and a green salad.

73

GOOD CATCH IN THE EVERGLADES   *Florida*

ROYAL POINCIANA STUFFED POMPANO

(Pompano, shrimp, mushrooms, eggs, cream, sherry)

This famous Florida recipe was especially created for pompano, but it can be used for many fish that yield firm, fine-textured fillets such as black sea bass, Great Lakes whitefish or salmon trout. Allow 2½ to 3 pounds of fillets to serve six.

Shell and devein 1 pound of boiled shrimp and put them through the finest blade of the meat grinder. Mix the shrimp with ½ cup of chopped mushrooms and 2 eggs beaten with ½ cup of cream and ¼ cup of sherry. Work the mixture to a smooth paste and season it with salt and pepper. Have the pompano split into two fillets and boned. Put one fillet into a shallow buttered baking dish, spread it with the shrimp stuffing, cover with the second fillet, and skewer them together with wooden toothpicks. Pour ½ cup of cream over the fish and bake it in a 350° oven for 45 minutes, basting often with the pan juices.

PACKET BOATS "SENATOR" AND "CAPITOL" *St. Louis, Missouri*

SQUAB IN SAUERKRAUT

(Squab, sauerkraut, chicken consommé, butter, spices, link sausages)

Wash 1½ pounds of sauerkraut very thoroughly under running water and squeeze it dry in a colander. Put it in a heavy saucepan with 2 cups of chicken consommé, 1 cup of water, 4 tablespoons of butter, 2 tablespoons of cider vinegar, a dozen juniper berries and 6 peppercorns. Simmer it, covered, for 2 hours, by which time the liquid should be almost gone.

Rub 6 squab inside and out with salt and pepper and tie a piece of bacon or salt pork over each breast. Put them in a roasting pan with 1 cup of chicken consommé, roast them in a 500° oven for 10 minutes, then lower the heat to 325° and roast them for another 35 minutes. Baste them often and remove the bacon when they are done.

Fry a dozen tiny link sausages and drain them on absorbent paper. Put the sauerkraut in a large ovenproof casserole, make a hollow in the center and arrange the roast squab on it. Surround them with the sausages and pour the roasting-pan juices, skimmed of most of their fat, over all. Cover the casserole and bake it at 325° for 15 minutes. Serves six.

BRATTLE STREET MANSION   *Cambridge, Massachusetts*

EMERSON BREAD

(Flour, lard, water, salt, sugar, yeast)

A very old recipe for homemade bread, and an easy one, as the dough does not have to be kneaded: In a large bowl dissolve 2 tablespoons of lard in 2 cups of boiling water. Add 2 cups of cold water, 2 tablespoons each of salt and sugar, and 1 yeast cake. Stir until salt, sugar and yeast are all dissolved. Add 9 cups of sifted flour, or a little more, to make a soft moist dough, and work it thoroughly with a wooden spoon. Leave it in a floured bowl, covered with a cloth and away from drafts, to rise until it is doubled in bulk; this will take anywhere from 3 to 8 hours, depending on the temperature. Punch the dough down, divide it into halves, or thirds, and put it in 2 or 3 greased bread pans. Let the dough rise until it doubles in bulk again. Bake the bread in a preheated 400° oven for 40 to 60 minutes, depending on the size of the loaves. Remove them from the pans and cool them on wire racks.

THE WENTWORTH-GARDNER HOUSE (1760) *Portsmouth, New Hampshire*

Eggplant with Clam Stuffing

(Eggplant, onion, bread crumbs, clams, egg, herbs, grated cheese)

Cut a large eggplant in half lengthwise and score the flesh with a few shallow slashes. Heat 4 tablespoons of oil in a large skillet and put in the eggplant halves, cut side down. Cover the skillet and cook the eggplant over a low flame for 15 to 20 minutes; then remove it and scoop out the flesh, leaving a ¼-inch layer on the skins to keep them whole.

Sauté 1 minced onion in 2 tablespoons of butter until it is soft. Add the eggplant, chopped, 1 cup of soft bread crumbs, 1 cup of minced clams with their juice (either fresh steamed ones or canned ones), 1 beaten egg, 2 tablespoons of minced parsley, ½ teaspoon of thyme, and salt and pepper to taste. Blend the mixture well and stuff the eggplant shells with it. Sprinkle the tops with bread crumbs and grated cheese, dot them generously with butter, and bake the stuffed eggplant in a 375° oven for 30 minutes. Serves four to six.

SUNLIT COTTAGE   *Wickford, Rhode Island*

Rhode Island Jonny Cake

(White water-ground corn meal, salt, boiling water, cream, bacon fat)

Use old-fashioned white water-ground corn meal which many New England country stores now sell by mail order. Mix 1 cup of meal and 1 teaspoon of salt, add slowly 1¼ to 1½ cups of boiling water to make a batter a little thicker than the usual pancake batter and beat it hard for 3 or 4 minutes. Add 3 table-spoons of heavy cream (not in the authentic recipe, but good for browning) and drop the batter by spoonfuls, quite far apart, on a hot griddle greased with bacon fat. Brown the cakes well on one side, flip them over with a wide spatula and brown the other side. If the jonny cakes are not *less* than ¼ inch thick, the batter is too heavy and needs more hot water. Serve hot, with butter, and with maple syrup if no native of Rhode Island is watching.

78

THE LIGHTHOUSE (1848)   *Biloxi, Mississippi*

HAM A LA KING

(Ham, green pepper, mushrooms, butter, cream, milk, egg yolks, pimientos, sherry)

This is simply the recipe for the original chicken à la King; but ham is an excellent variation. In a skillet sauté 1 small green pepper, minced, and ½ pound of sliced mushrooms in 2 tablespoons of butter until they are soft but not brown. Meanwhile, in the top of a double boiler, make a cream sauce by blending 2 tablespoons of flour into 3 tablespoons of melted butter and adding gradually 1 cup each of milk and thin cream. Cook the sauce over medium heat, stirring constantly, until it is smooth and thickened. Mix a little of this sauce with 2 lightly beaten egg yolks, return the mixture to the sauce, and add 2 cups of diced cooked ham, the sautéed mushrooms and peppers, ½ cup of diced pimientos, 1 teaspoon of lemon juice, 2 tablespoons of sherry, and salt and pepper to taste. Stir the ham à la King over hot water until the sauce reaches the proper consistency, and serve it with rice, on toast, or in heated patty shells. Serves six.

79

WHEAT FIELDS
in the Wind River Basin

near Lander, Wyoming

Steak and Kidney Pie

(Round steak, lamb kidneys, onions, carrot, herbs, beef bouillon, pastry)

Trim the fat from a 2-pound piece of round steak, cut the meat into cubes and roll them lightly in flour seasoned with salt and pepper. Heat 2 tablespoons of the beef fat in a Dutch oven and brown the pieces of steak in it. Add 3 medium onions, quartered, or 10 tiny whole ones, 1 large carrot, sliced, ½ teaspoon of thyme, 1 bay leaf, a dash of Worcestershire, and 3½ cups of hot beef bouillon. Cover the stew and simmer it for 1½ hours, or until the meat is tender.

Meanwhile, split 4 lamb kidneys lengthwise, discard their tubes, gristle and fat, and put them to soak in cold water for 45 minutes. Prepare your favorite recipe for rich pie pastry and chill it. When the beef is tender, thicken the sauce with 2 tablespoons of flour creamed with 1 tablespoon of butter. Then drain the lamb kidneys, cut them in ½-inch dice and sauté them briefly in a little butter. Add them to the beef and transfer the stew to a baking dish. Roll out the pastry and cut a ½-inch circle out of the center. Put the pastry over the stew, trim the edges, decorate it with the scraps cut in fancy shapes, and brush it with beaten egg or milk. Bake the pie in a 450° oven for 10 minutes, then lower the heat to 350° and bake it another 20 minutes. Serves six.

MANHATTAN AT TWILIGHT   *New York City*
from the RCA Building

CASSEROLE SQUIRE

(Chicken, onion, rice, consommé, saffron, tomato paste, ham, shrimp, mushrooms)

Cut a broiler into small serving pieces and discard the wing tips and the bony pieces of the back. In a heavy casserole brown the chicken well in 2 tablespoons of hot butter. Remove the chicken, add 2 more tablespoons of butter to the casserole and in it sauté 1 medium onion, chopped, until it is golden. Add 1½ cups of Carolina rice and stir until every grain is coated. Then stir in 1½ cups of chicken consommé, ⅜ teaspoon of saffron first soaked in a spoonful of the consommé, and 1½ teaspoons of tomato paste. From this point on, the cooking must be over a very low flame (an asbestos mat helps) and the casserole must always be covered. Cook the rice until the liquid is almost gone, then add the chicken and another 3½ cups of consommé, and cook for another 15 minutes. Finally, add 1 cup of coarsely diced ham, 1 pound of shrimp, boiled, shelled and deveined, and ½ pound of sliced mushrooms sautéed briefly in a little butter. Stir everything together well, taste for seasoning, and continue cooking until all the liquid is absorbed. Serves six to eight.

"VIZCAYA"   *near Miami, Florida*

TROPICAL ICE

(Mangoes or peaches, sugar, lime juice, orange juice, preserved kumquats, liqueur)

Mangoes are called for, but perfectly ripe yellow peaches will be as delicious, if not as exotic. Make a syrup by boiling together 2 cups of water and 1 cup of sugar for 5 minutes, and chill it. Set the refrigerator controls at "very cold." In a potato ricer crush enough peeled and pitted ripe mangoes or peaches to make 2 cups of pulp. Add ½ cup of lime juice, 1 cup of orange juice, and the chilled syrup, pour the mixture into a deep refrigerator tray, and place it in the freezer compartment. When the ice reaches the mushy stage, spoon it into a bowl and beat it hard with an egg beater. Return it to the tray, freeze it again, beat it again, then leave it to freeze for at least 3 hours with a piece of waxed paper pressed firmly over the top. Makes about 1½ quarts. Serve with kumquats preserved in syrup; split the kumquats lengthwise with a sharp pointed knife, seed them, and add a little orange liqueur to the syrup.

SEPTEMBER "DOWN EAST"   *near Sabbatus, Maine*

BAKED GREEN CORN

(Fresh corn, butter, cream)

With a sharp knife score each row of kernels on 12 ears of fresh corn, then scrape off all the pulp with the dull side of the knife; or use a special corn scraper that will do the job more easily. Add to the corn: salt, pepper, 1 teaspoon of sugar, 4 tablespoons of butter cut in small pieces, and 6 tablespoons of cream. If the corn is very young and juicy, you will need to add 1 teaspoon of cornstarch, blended with the cream, to thicken the mixture; or, if it is quite mature, you will need ½ cup or more of cream to dilute it. Mix well and pour the corn into a buttered baking dish. Bake it in a 325° oven for 1 hour, or until the sides and top are brown and crisp. Serves four.

HERBERT HOOVER'S BIRTHPLACE *West Branch, Iowa*

GOLDEN BUCK

(American cheese, butter, cream, mustard, cayenne, eggs, toast)

While making the cheese sauce, have 6 eggs poaching in an egg poacher and toast 6 slices of bread in the oven until crisp. Meanwhile, in the top of a double boiler, over barely simmering water, melt 1 tablespoon of butter and 1½ cups of grated sharp American cheese. Stir often and when the cheese is melted, add ½ to ¾ cup of cream mixed with 1 beaten egg. Season with ½ teaspoon of dry mustard, a touch of cayenne, and salt to taste. Cook the sauce a little longer, still stirring, and remove it from the heat the instant it is properly thickened. Butter the hot toast, cover it with cheese sauce and top with the poached eggs. Sprinkle the eggs with paprika and serve immediately.

THE STATE CAPITOL   *Charleston, West Virginia*

APPLE BROWN BETTY

(Apples, brown sugar, spices, lemon, bread crumbs, butter)

Peel, core and slice thinly enough tart apples to make 1½ pints. Sift together ¾ cup of brown sugar, ½ teaspoon of cinnamon, and ¼ teaspoon each of salt, nutmeg, and clove, then add the grated rind of half a lemon. Mix 1½ cups of fine bread crumbs with ¼ cup of melted butter and spread one-third of this mixture on the bottom of a buttered baking dish. Put half the sliced apples in the dish, pour 1 tablespoon of lemon juice over them, then sprinkle in half the spiced sugar and half the remaining buttered crumbs. Add the rest of the apples, another tablespoon of lemon juice, ½ cup of water, and all the remaining brown sugar and crumbs. Bake the apple Betty, covered, in a 350° oven for about 40 minutes, or until the apples are almost tender; then remove the cover and bake the dish for 15 minutes, or until the top is golden brown and the juice is reduced. Serve hot, with heavy cream or with maple foamy sauce (see *Index*). Serves four to six.

PRE-REVOLUTIONARY TAVERN   *Fairfield, Connecticut*

SAUTEED SUMMER SQUASH

(Summer squash, onions, mushrooms or green pepper, herbs, butter, olive oil, lemon)

Cook 1 cup each of thinly sliced sweet onion and fresh mushrooms in 2 table-spoons each of butter and olive oil until they are soft but not brown. Add ¼ teaspoon of crushed rosemary and 2 or 3 small yellow summer squash (about 1 pound), washed and sliced but not peeled. Season the vegetables with salt and pepper and simmer them covered, for 5 to 10 minutes, or until the squash is tender. Serve sprinkled with lemon juice and chopped parsley. The same recipe, with quite a different flavor, can be made by substituting ½ cup of diced green pepper for the mushrooms and orégano for the rosemary. Serves four.

86

BEGINNERS' SLOPE
"Little Nell"

Aspen, Colorado

BORSCH

(Beets, onion, tomatoes, garlic, dill, beef broth, gelatin, sour cream)

Melt 2 tablespoons of butter in a soup kettle and add 3 cups of coarsely grated raw beets and 1 tablespoon of vinegar. Stir well and add 1 chopped onion, 2 small tomatoes, peeled, seeded and chopped, 1 clove of garlic stuck with a wooden toothpick, and several sprigs of fresh dill. Simmer the vegetables together for 15 minutes, then add 6 cups of beef broth, and salt, pepper, lemon juice, and a little sugar, to taste. Cover the kettle, cook the soup over low heat for 30 minutes, then turn off the heat and let it steep for several hours. Remove the garlic, reheat the borsch, and serve it in soup bowls with a sauceboat of sour cream.

Or to serve cold: Strain the soup and discard the vegetables, or purée it all, 2 cups at a time, in an electric blender. For 6 cups of borsch, soak 3 tablespoons of gelatin in another ½ cup of the soup. Reheat the soup, add the gelatin mixture, and stir until it is dissolved. Cool the borsch before storing it in the refrigerator. When it has jelled, chop it coarsely with a fork, put it in chilled consommé cups, and top each serving with sour cream and minced fresh dill. Serves six to eight.

THE RINGLING MUSEUM   *Sarasota, Florida*

Avocado Cream Sturgis

(Avocados, lime juice, powdered sugar, crème de cacao)

A fabulous tropical dessert: Cut 2 large avocados in half and scoop out the pulp. Purée it in an electric blender with the juice of 4 small limes and 6 tablespoons of powdered sugar. Chill the avocado cream in individual ramekins and pour a spoonful of crème de cacao over each one just before serving. Serves six.

ROADSIDE SCENE   *North Woodstock, Connecticut*

MUSHROOM KETCHUP

(Mushrooms, onion, cider vinegar, horseradish, spices)

Trim the stem ends of 5 pounds of mushrooms. Wipe each mushroom with a damp cloth; do not peel or wash them. Chop them rather fine. Put 2 bay leaves in a bowl, add the mushrooms and sprinkle them with 4 tablespoons of salt. Cover them and let them stand overnight. Next day, remove the bay leaves and crush the mushrooms with a wooden potato masher. Add 1 medium onion, minced, ½ teaspoon each of ground cloves, allspice and grated horseradish, ⅛ teaspoon of cayenne pepper, the grated rind of 1 lemon, the bay leaves, and ½ cup of cider vinegar. Bring the mixture to a boil and simmer it for 30 minutes, stirring often. Then discard the bay leaves and rub the ketchup through a sieve. It should be a little thinner than the usual tomato ketchup; add a little hot vinegar if it is too thick. Reheat the ketchup to the boiling point and seal it in hot sterilized jars. Serve with cold meats or use to season stews and sauces. Makes about 1½ pints.

MAROON BELLS MOUNTAINS *Colorado*

Chilled Poached Trout

(Trout, cider vinegar, onion, carrot, herbs, spices, eggs, sour cream, cucumber)

In a large shallow pan simmer together for 30 minutes 1½ quarts of water, ¾ cup of cider vinegar, 1 onion stuck with 3 cloves, 1 sliced carrot, 2 slices of lemon, 1 bay leaf, a good pinch of thyme, several sprigs of parsley, 4 crushed peppercorns, and ½ teaspoon of salt. Poach 4 small whole, cleaned trout in this bouillon, at a very low simmer, for 5 minutes, or until they are just cooked through. Remove them carefully, drain them on a cloth, let them cool, and chill them in the refrigerator. Shortly before servingtime, arrange them on a platter and remove the skin from the top sides. Slice 4 hard-boiled eggs, arrange the center slices, overlapping neatly, on the trout, and sprinkle them with chopped fresh dill and chives. Serve the trout with a sauce made of 1 cup of sour cream, ⅓ cup of finely chopped cucumber, squeezed dry in a cloth, the remaining slices of hard-boiled egg, also finely chopped, 1 tablespoon each of minced fresh dill and chives, and lemon juice, salt and white pepper to taste. Serves four.

THE COLORADO RIVER
from Dead Horse Point

near Crescent Junction, Utah

CHINESE SPINACH

(Spinach, salad oil, garlic, ginger, cornstarch, sherry, soy sauce)

Wash 2 pounds of tender young spinach, break off the stems and cut the leaves into 2-inch pieces. Heat 3 tablespoons of salad oil in a large skillet and add 1 minced and crushed clove of garlic and 1 teaspoon of finely minced fresh ginger. (Candied ginger, thoroughly scrubbed in water to remove the sugar, will do, though it will remain a little sweet.) Add the spinach and toss it well in the oil so all the leaves will be coated. Add 1 teaspoon of cornstarch dissolved in ¼ cup of sherry, 1 teaspoon of soy sauce, and salt and pepper. Stir again thoroughly, cover the saucepan and cook the spinach over fairly high heat for 3 minutes. Serve without draining or chopping, with butterfly shrimp (see *Index*) and boiled rice. Serves six.

CHERRY BLOSSOMS BELOW MT. HOOD   *Oregon*

BLACK CHERRY PRESERVES

(Black cherries, sugar, lemon juice)

Measure 4 cups of pitted sweet black cherries, mix them with 2 cups of sugar and let them stand for 2 or 3 hours. In a large saucepan dissolve 1½ cups of sugar in ½ cup of water, bring the syrup to a boil and boil it for 5 minutes. Add ¼ cup of lemon juice and the sweetened cherries and cook them over a good flame for 15 minutes, or until they are translucent and the juice is thickened. If you use a candy thermometer, the preserves are ready to take off the fire when it registers 222°. Let the preserves stand overnight and seal cold.

92

GHOST TOWN

Virginia City, Montana

BOILED TONGUE WITH RAISIN SAUCE

(Tongue, butter, gingersnaps, cider, raisins, almonds, lemon, spices)

Simmer a well-scrubbed fresh beef tongue for 2 to 3 hours in water to cover with 2 onions, 1 carrot, 2 stalks of celery, 6 peppercorns, 3 whole cloves, 1 bay leaf, and 2 teaspoons of salt. When the tongue is tender, skin it carefully and cut away the fat and gristle at the root. Arrange it, thinly sliced, on a platter, surround it with buttered noodles and serve it with raisin sauce:

Soak enough gingersnaps to a pulp in a little boiling water to make ¼ cup when the water is squeezed out. Heat 4 tablespoons of butter in a heavy saucepan until it browns, but do not let it smoke. Stir in gradually 1½ cups of the tongue stock and ½ cup of cider or cooking sherry. Add ⅔ cup of seedless raisins, ½ cup of blanched slivered almonds, 6 paper-thin slices of lemon, quartered and seeded, and a pinch each of cinnamon and clove. Stir in the gingersnaps, season the sauce to taste with salt and pepper and simmer it slowly, stirring often, for about 30 minutes or until the raisins are plump and the liquid is smooth and a little reduced.

BEACON STREET   *Boston, Massachusetts*

Miss Parloa's Turkey-Hominy Croquettes (1887)

(Hominy, turkey or ham, onion, butter, milk, parsley, eggs, bread crumbs)

In a saucepan sauté 1 tablespoon of minced onion in 2 teaspoons of butter until it is soft. Add ½ cup of milk, and stir in 1 cup of boiled hominy grits, 1 cup of finely ground meat, preferably cold roast turkey or ham, 2 tablespoons each of butter and chopped parsley, salt to taste, and a generous grinding of black pepper. Stir the mixture well and when it is heated through, remove it from the fire and add 1 beaten egg. Cook for another minute, stirring constantly, and spread the mixture on a platter to cool. When it is firm, shape it into cylinders about 3 inches long, roll them in beaten egg and bread crumbs, and fry them in hot deep fat until they are golden brown. Makes 8 to 10 croquettes.

RANCH IN THE BADLANDS   *North Dakota*

Swedish Cabbage Rolls

(Cabbage, ground meat, rice, egg, onion, brown sugar, bouillon, sour cream)

Core the stem end of a cabbage, put it in boiling salted water to cover, and cook it until the outside leaves separate easily, about 15 minutes. Drain it, peel off 8 large perfect leaves and trim off their thick center veins.

Mix together ⅓ pound each of ground beef, veal and pork, 1 cup of cooked rice, 1 egg beaten with ¼ cup of cream, 2 tablespoons of minced parsley, and 1 onion, minced and sautéed in butter until soft. Season with salt, pepper and nutmeg. Divide the stuffing between the 8 cabbage leaves. Fold the sides of the leaves over their stuffing, roll them up, and pin the overlapping ends with wooden toothpicks. In an ovenproof casserole brown the cabbage rolls lightly on all sides in 2 tablespoons of hot butter. Then sprinkle them with 2 tablespoons of brown sugar, add 2 cups of beef bouillon and bake them, covered, in a 350° oven for 1 hour, basting often. Remove the rolls to a hot serving dish. Stir ½ cup of sour cream into the casserole and simmer the sauce for 2 or 3 minutes. Taste it for seasoning, pour it over the cabbage rolls and dust with paprika. Serves four.

LATE SUMMER AFTERNOON   *Kansas*

Green Corn Soup

(Fresh corn, milk, cream, butter, flour, egg yolks)

Grate the kernels, raw, from 8 ears of fresh young corn. In a soup kettle boil 4 or 5 of the cobs in 1 quart of water or chicken stock for 45 minutes; remove them and add the corn kernels to the kettle. Simmer the corn for 10 minutes, then add 1 quart of milk and ½ cup of cream, heat well, and stir in 4 tablespoons of butter creamed with 2 tablespoons of flour. Season the soup well with salt and pepper and simmer it for another 5 minutes. Just before serving, combine a little of the hot soup with 2 beaten egg yolks, stir the mixture gradually into the soup and serve immediately. Serves six to eight.

SLATER'S MILL   *Pawtucket, Rhode Island*

GREEN SALAD CAROLINE

(Lettuce, raw cauliflower, green pepper, avocado, French dressing, herbs)

Rub a wooden salad bowl with a cut clove of garlic. In it arrange the leaves of a head of green garden lettuce, washed, drained and patted dry with a cloth. Over the lettuce sprinkle 1 cup of small raw cauliflowerets and 1 green pepper cut in thin strips. The salad bowl can then be left to chill in the refrigerator until servingtime. Just before serving, peel, halve, and slice thinly 1 ripe avocado. Add it to the salad and pour on ½ cup of French dressing made with 1 part wine vinegar, 3 parts olive oil, and salt, pepper and prepared mustard to taste. Add a sprinkling of minced fresh parsley and chives and toss the salad at the table. Serves six.

THE PIRATE'S HOUSE   *Charleston, South Carolina*

CHICKEN SHORTCAKE

(Chicken, herbs, butter, flour, mushrooms)

Put a 6-pound chicken in a soup kettle with cold water to cover and 1 onion, 2 stalks of celery, parsley, thyme, 1 bay leaf and 2 teaspoons of salt. Bring the water to a boil, skim it once or twice, and simmer the chicken very slowly for 1½ hours. Take out the chicken, strain the broth, let it cool, and skim off the fat and reserve it. Remove the skin and bones from the chicken and cut the meat into cubes.

Trim the stems from 1 pound of button mushrooms and sauté the caps gently in butter and until they are lightly browned but not shriveled. In a saucepan melt 3 tablespoons each of chicken fat and butter, blend in 5 tablespoons of flour, stir in gradually 4 cups of the chicken broth and simmer the sauce, stirring often, until it thickens. Add the chicken and the mushrooms, taste for seasoning, and cook a few minutes longer. Split large, piping hot baking powder biscuits (see *Index*) and arrange the bottoms on a heated platter. Spoon the chicken mixture over them, cover with the biscuit tops, pour on a little more sauce and sprinkle with minced parsley. Serves six to eight.

98

RED MESA CLIFFS *near Gallup, New Mexico*

Colache

(Squash, bacon fat, onion, green peppers, tomatoes, garlic, chili, corn)

Cut into 1-inch dice 4 small summer squash and 4 zucchini, or use whatever squash are available, winter or summer, even a piece of pumpkin. There should be about 1 quart of diced vegetable. Melt 2 tablespoons each of bacon fat and butter in a large casserole, add the squash and cook it for about 5 minutes, stirring to brown the pieces lightly on all sides. Add 1 large onion and 2 green peppers, all chopped, and sauté all together for 2 or 3 minutes. Then add 2 cups of Italian plum tomatoes, 1 minced clove of garlic, 1 teaspoon of chili powder (1 minced chili pepper is, of course, better if available), and season well with salt and pepper. Simmer the mixture, covered, for 20 minutes, then add the kernels of 4 ears of corn freshly scraped from the cobs and cook the colache for another 10 minutes, or until all the vegetables are tender. Serves six.

Univ. of Arizona Library

OYSTER FISHERMAN'S CAMP   *Barataria Bay, Louisiana*

OYSTERS POULETTE

(Oysters, butter, cream, egg yolks, cayenne, lemon juice, whipped cream)

Heat 1 pint of oysters in their liquor until the edges begin to curl. Skim the liquid carefully, drain the oysters and reserve the liquid. In a saucepan blend 1 tablespoon of flour into 1 tablespoon of melted butter and gradually stir in the oyster liquor, about ¾ cup, mixed with ¾ cup of cream. Thicken the sauce slowly, stirring constantly, season it with pepper, cayenne, and a little salt to taste, and take the saucepan off the fire.

In the top of a double boiler beat 2 egg yolks with ¼ cup of cream. Add a little of the cream sauce, blend well, and add the rest of the sauce. Cook over simmering water, still stirring, until the eggs just begin to thicken, then add 1 teaspoon of lemon juice and the oysters. Pour the mixture into a warm serving dish and top it with a little whipped cream. The perfect garnish for oysters poulette is a circle of puff-paste crescents, but small baking powder biscuit (see *Index*) or triangles of toast will do nicely also. Serves six.

RIDE ON THE RANGE   *Bandera County, Texas*

Tamale Pie

(Corn meal, vegetables, ground beef, tomatoes, olives, coriander, chili)

In the top of a large double boiler scald 1 cup of corn meal with 1 cup of boiling water and mix well. White water-ground meal is best, but yellow will do. Stir in 1 quart of boiling salted water, or beef stock, and cook the mush over boiling water, stirring occasionally, until it is well thickened. Line a deep buttered baking dish with two-thirds of the mush and let it cool.

In a skillet sauté 1 large onion, chopped, in 2 tablespoons of olive oil until it is soft. Add ¼ cup of chopped green pepper and 1 minced clove of garlic, and simmer the mixture 2 or 3 minutes. Add 1 pound of lean ground beef, cook it briefly, stirring, until it crumbles and loses its color, than add 2 cups of Italian plum tomatoes and ¼ cup of pitted and minced ripe olives. Season this stuffing with 1 teaspoon of ground coriander, salt and 1 to 3 tablespoons of chili powder to taste, and simmer it for 10 minutes. Transfer it to the baking dish and cover with the reserved corn meal mush. Pour melted butter over the top of the pie and bake it in a 350° oven for 45 minutes. Serves six.

BOURBON STREET *New Orleans, Louisiana*

Cafe Brulot

(Coffee, brandy, lemon and orange rind, sugar, cinnamon stick, cloves)

Use a brûlot bowl, or a silver bowl first rinsed in boiling water, or a chafing dish. Have ready in a pot 1½ pints of very strong hot coffee. Put in the bowl the thin outer rinds of 1 lemon and 1 orange, 6 lumps of sugar, 4 whole cloves and a piece of cinnamon stick, and add ¾ to 1½ cups of brandy. (The amount of brandy is a matter of taste, as some recipes call for only 2 or 3 jiggers.) Warm a small silver ladle with a match, scoop up some of the brandy, put 2 lumps of sugar in it, and light it. Lower the ladle into the bowl to ignite the rest of the brandy, then slowly pour in the hot coffee. Blend the mixture by dipping the ladle back and forth gently so as not to extinguish the flames too soon. Serve in demitasses as soon as the flame goes out. Serves eight to ten.

MILL ON CONESTOGA CREEK *near Lancaster, Pennsylvania*

LETTUCE AND SCALLION SOUP

(Lettuce, scallions, bacon fat, curry, herbs, chicken broth, cream, egg)

Shred finely 1 medium head of green garden lettuce, and mince 8 scallions with the tender part of their green tops. In a saucepan sauté the scallions in 3 tablespoons of bacon fat until they are soft, but do not let them brown. Add the shredded lettuce, 1 teaspoon of curry powder, ¼ teaspoon of dried tarragon, and 1 cup of hot chicken broth. Stir well and simmer, covered, for 4 or 5 minutes, or until the lettuce is wilted and tender. Then purée the soup in an electric blender, return it to the saucepan, and add 1 cup of thin cream. Taste for seasoning, bring the soup to a boil, and serve with 1 slice of hard-boiled egg and a sprinkling of chopped chives floated on each serving. Serves four.

103

THE MANSE
Home of Woodrow Wilson

Staunton, Virginia

Mint-Barbecued Lamb

(Lamb, mint marinade, sweet red peppers, bacon)

Crush together 1 medium onion and 1 clove of garlic, both minced, ½ teaspoon of rosemary, 8 peppercorns, ½ teaspoon of salt, and a dozen chopped fresh mint leaves. Use a mortar and pestle to do this, or a heavy bowl and a wooden potato masher. Add ½ teaspoon of sweet Bahamian mustard and, bit by bit, ¼ cup of olive oil, and work the mixture to a smooth paste. Add 1 cup of dry sherry and 2 tablespoons of cider vinegar, and beat the marinade well with a fork. Put 2½ pounds of lean tender lamb, cut in 1½-inch cubes, in a bowl, add the marinade, and marinate the meat, covered, for 8 to 24 hours, turning it several times. Thread the cubes of lamb on skewers, alternating them with squares of sliced bacon and sweet red pepper. Broil them under a high flame, basting often with the marinade, until the meat is well browned but still pink in the center. Serves six.

TWIN SILOS   *near Middleton, Maryland*

Buffet Party Cole Slaw

(Cabbage, seasonings, vinegar, egg yolks, butter, sweet and sour cream, radishes)

In the top of a double boiler mix together 1 teaspoon of salt, 1 tablespoon each of sugar and flour, ½ teaspoon of celery seed and a generous grinding of black pepper. Blend into this ½ cup of cider vinegar, diluted with 3 or 4 tablespoons of water, 1 teaspoon of prepared mustard, 2 tablespoons of grated onion, and 4 well-beaten egg yolks. Cook the dressing over barely simmering water and stir it with a wire whisk until it just begins to thicken. Add 4 tablespoons of butter, cut in pieces, and keep stirring until the butter is melted and the dressing thickens like a rich hollandaise. Remove it immediately from the heat, cool it, then add ½ cup each of heavy sweet cream and sour cream. Reserve ¾ cup of dressing. Mix the rest with about 2 quarts of finely shredded cabbage and put the cole slaw in a glass bowl. Pat the top smooth, mask it with the reserved dressing, sprinkle generously with chopped fresh dill, and plant a dozen radish roses around the edge. Serves twelve.

105

HARBOR BELOW DEVIL'S THUMB PEAK   *Petersburg, Alaska*

KASHA

(Buckwheat groats, egg, chicken stock, mushrooms, onions, raisins, almonds)

A Russian specialty that takes the place on the menu of potatoes or rice. It can be served plain with butter or chicken fat, or elaborated with one or all of the following: ¼ pound of sliced fresh mushrooms sautéed in butter; 1 onion, chopped and sautéed in butter; ½ cup of seedless raisins plumped in a little boiling water and drained; and ½ cup of blanched slivered almonds. Kasha with these added ingredients also makes an excellent stuffing for furred or feathered game.

In a bowl mix together 1 egg and 1½ cups of buckwheat groats. Transfer the mixture to a large skillet and stir it briskly over a high flame for 2 or 3 minutes until each grain is separate. Add 3 cups of boiling chicken stock and salt and pepper, cover the skillet, lower the heat, and cook the kasha for 20 to 30 minutes; the time depends on the coarseness of the grain. Stir occasionally and add a little boiling stock if necessary. When it is done the kasha should be dry and fluffy, never mushy. Add 4 tablespoons of butter or chicken fat, or the sautéed vegetables and the raisins and nuts, 5 minutes before the cooking time is up. Serves six.

106

AUTUMN AFTERNOON   *Hancock, New Hampshire*

WILD-RICE STUFFING FOR DUCK AND GAME BIRDS

(Wild rice, onion, mushrooms, green pepper, duck liver, walnuts, herbs, brandy)

Wash 1 cup of wild rice thoroughly, stir it into 1 quart of boiling salted water and cook it for 30 to 35 minutes, or until it is almost tender. Meanwhile, sauté 1 chopped onion in 4 tablespoons of butter until it is soft. Add 1 small can of button mushrooms, drained, and ¼ cup of minced green pepper, and simmer the vegetables another 3 or 4 minutes. Drain the rice, return it to the saucepan and shake it over a low flame to dry it. Combine the rice, the sautéed vegetables, the chopped raw liver of the bird, ½ cup of coarsely chopped walnut meats, 1½ tablespoons each of minced parsley and celery leaves, and 1 teaspoon of marjoram. Season the stuffing with salt and freshly ground pepper, moisten it with 1 tablespoon of brandy and the liquor from the can of mushrooms, and let it cool before stuffing the bird. Enough to stuff loosely a 5- to 6-pound duck.

THE WHITE CITY   *Miami, Florida*

Chicken Soup with Matzo Balls

(Stewing hen, vegetables, eggs, chicken fat, matzo meal)

Put a large stewing hen in a soup kettle with 2½ quarts of cold water and 2 chicken feet, washed and scraped. Bring the water to a boil and simmer the hen, covered, for 1 hour, skimming the broth several times. Then add 1 onion, 3 stalks of celery, 2 carrots, 1 leek, several sprigs of parsley, and 2 teaspoons of salt, and simmer the soup for another 2 hours, or until it is very flavorful and the hen is tender. Strain the soup, cool it and skim off the fat. Use the hen, which will have relinquished most of its flavor, for some other, well-spiced dish such as a chicken curry or a salad.

Combine 3 well-beaten eggs, 3 tablespoons of melted chicken fat, 1 tablespoon of chopped parsley, and ½ teaspoon of salt. Add ½ to ⅔ cup of matzo meal, or enough to make a very soft dough, and chill it until it is firm. Then form the matzo mixture into ¾-inch balls, bring the chicken soup to a rolling boil and drop them in. Lower the heat and simmer the soup for another 10 to 15 minutes. Serves six.

108

THOMAS JEFFERSON'S MONTICELLO   *Charlottesville, Virginia*

Ambrosia

(Oranges, fresh coconut, sherry)

A Christmas-season dessert in the old south that lives up to its name even better on a hot summer day. Peel, slice thinly, and seed 8 sweet oranges, sprinkle a little sugar over them, and save all the juice. Grate enough fresh coconut to make 1½ to 2 cups. In a glass bowl arrange the slices in alternating layers with the coconut (other fruit, such as sliced bananas and whole strawberries can be added, too), and finish with a layer of coconut. Add the-reserved orange juice and ½ cup of good sherry and chill the ambrosia, tightly covered, before serving. In summertime, decorate it with fresh mint leaves. Serves six.

RANCH BELOW THE FLORIDA MOUNTAINS   *near Deming, New Mexico*

MEXICAN SALSA FRIA (Cold Sauce)

(Red and green tomatoes, onion, green chilis, garlic, coriander, oil, vinegar)

Chop finely and combine 4 large ripe tomatoes and 2 small green tomatoes, all peeled, 1 large sweet onion, and one 4-ounce can of peeled green chilis. Add 1 clove of garlic, minced and crushed, 3 tablespoons each of olive oil and wine vinegar, 2 teaspoons of minced fresh coriander (Chinese parsley), and salt and pepper to taste. If green chilis are not available, use 1 minced green pepper and add Tabasco and chili powder to taste; 1 teaspoon of dried orégano can be substituted for the fresh coriander. Serve very cold, with cold or charcoal-broiled meats.

110

THE LAW OFFICES OF JAMES MONROE   *Fredericksburg, Virginia*

Baked Hen Bethany

(Stewing hen, herbs, corn bread, white bread, onions, celery, milk, lemon)

Put a fat 5- to 6-pound stewing hen in a kettle with water to cover well, the giblets, 1 onion, quartered, a few celery leaves, a pinch of thyme, 6 peppercorns, and 2 teaspoons of salt. Bring the liquid to a boil and simmer the hen, covered, for 1½ hours, or until it is tender.

Crumble enough corn bread and stale white bread to make 3 cups of each, combine them and add 1½ cups of finely diced celery and 1 cup of chopped onion. When the hen is tender, transfer it to a large shallow baking dish. Skim the fat from the stock and reserve it. Moisten the corn-bread mixture with 1½ cups of stock, season it well with salt and freshly ground pepper, and stuff the hen loosely with part of it. Arrange the remaining stuffing in the dish around the bird, and brush the skin of the hen well with the reserved fat. Bake the hen in a 300° oven for 1 to 1½ hours, or until the skin is brown and crisp and the stuffing is crusty. Meanwhile, simmer the remaining stock slowly for 1 hour. In a saucepan blend 2 tablespoons of flour with a spoonful of stock. Add gradually 2 cups of stock and 1 cup of rich milk. Add the minced giblets of the hen, simmer the gravy, stirring occasionally, until it is slightly thickened, and season it well with salt, pepper, and a little lemon juice. Serves six.

111

CIGAR JOE   *Gloucester, Massachusetts*

Codfish Cakes

(Salt cod, potatoes, egg, butter)

Wash ½ pound of salt cod in cold water, shred it fine with two forks or cut it into very small pieces with scissors; there should be about 1 cup. Soak the fish in water for 2 hours. Peel and dice enough raw potatoes to make 2½ cups. Drain the fish and cook it with the potatoes in boiling water to cover until the potatoes are done but not mushy. Drain off the water, return the pan to the heat and shake it back and forth until the mixture is quite dry. Mash the fish and potatoes togther well and beat the mixture with a spoon until it is fluffy. Add 1 tablespoon of butter, 1 egg beaten with a spoonful of milk, and a little pepper, and beat another 5 minutes. Pan fry large spoonfuls of batter in butter, turn the cakes once to brown them on both sides, and serve them with tomato sauce. Or shape the batter into balls with a spoon and brown them in hot deep fat. Serves six. For cocktail hors-d'oeuvre shape the balls with a small teaspoon and serve them on toothpicks with tomato ketchup.

AUTUMN LEAVES   *Orford, New Hampshire*

Pumpkin Ice Cream Cake

(Pumpkin, pecans, spices, milk, sugar, gingersnaps, butter, whipped cream)

Combine 1 cup of cooked pumpkin purée (canned, if you wish, but un-seasoned), ½ cup of chopped pecans, ½ teaspoon of cinnamon, ¼ teaspoon of nutmeg, ⅛ teaspoon of salt, and ½ cup of sugar dissolved completely in ½ cup of hot milk. Beat the mixture well with a spoon and chill it.

Blend 6 tablespoons of melted butter into 1½ cups of fine gingersnap crumbs and line a ring mold with the mixture, pressing it firmly against the bottom and sides. Whip 1 cup of heavy cream and fold it into the chilled pumpkin. Spoon the pumpkin cream into the gingersnap crust, decorate the top of the cake with pecan halves, and put it in the freezing compartment of the refrigerator until it is set but not hard. To serve, wipe the sides of the mold with a cloth wrung out of very hot water and take off the ring. Serves six.

THE WOODSHED   *Lower Waterford, Vermont*

Rhubarb Crumble

(Rhubarb, granulated sugar, brown sugar, orange rind, flour, butter, cinnamon)

Dice enough young rhubarb to make 4 cups and mix it with 1½ cups of granulated sugar, or more if the rhubarb is very tart, and the grated rind of half an orange. Put the rhubarb in a well-buttered 9-inch glass pie plate. In a bowl cut together with two knives (as you would ordinary pastry ingredients) 1 cup of brown sugar, 1 cup of sifted flour, ½ cup of butter, and 1 teaspoon of cinnamon until the mixture crumbles evenly. These are the proportions of the original recipe and they make a thick topping. They may be cut down by one-third if you wish, but become sparse if you cut down by a full half. Spread the crumbled mixture evenly over the rhubarb and bake the dish in a 375° oven for 30 minutes, or until the rhubarb is bright red and soft. Serve warm or cold, with heavy cream or whipped cream. Better known is the same recipe for apple crumble; for this use tart cooking apples, sliced and sprinkled sparingly with sugar, cinnamon and lemon juice. Serves four to six.

THE VILLAGE CHURCH *Colebrook, Connecticut*

Onion Souffle

(White onions, butter, flour, milk, cayenne pepper, eggs)

Make 1 cup of onion purée by boiling half a dozen large white onions in salted water until they are quite soft. Drain them, chop them fine or force them through a sieve. Add salt, pepper and 1 tablespoon of butter.

Make a cream sauce with 4 tablespoons of melted butter, 4 tablespoons of flour blended in smoothly, 1 cup of milk added gradually, and salt, pepper and a touch of cayenne. Simmer this sauce, stirring often, until it is thick and creamy, then stir in the cup of onion purée. Take the pan off the fire, let it cool a little and stir in gradually 4 well-beaten egg yolks.

Beat 6 egg whites stiff but not dry and fold one-third of them carefully but thoroughly into the cream-sauce mixture; then fold in the rest lightly and pour the batter into a buttered baking dish. (The dish should not be more than three-quarters full.) Bake the soufflé in a preheated 350° oven for about 40 minutes, or until it is puffed high and delicately browned. Serve immediately, of course. Serves four to six.

THE ORIGINAL FIRST PRESBYTERIAN CHURCH   *Wilmington, Delaware*
Brandywine Park

Herb Garden Baked Eggs

(Fresh herbs, eggs, butter, cream, grated cheese)

Use for this 3 generous tablespoons of mixed chopped fresh herbs, whichever ones are available—thyme, tarragon, basil, etc., and parsley; or use 3 teaspoons of mixed dried herbs, steep them for a minute or two in 2 tablespoons of boiling water, drain them, and combine them with 1 tablespoon of fresh minced parsley. Slice 6 hard-boiled eggs and arrange them in a shallow buttered baking dish. In the top of a double boiler, over direct heat, melt 2 tablespoons of butter, add the herbs and simmer them just enough to wilt them. Put the pan over hot water and stir in 1 cup of cream mixed with 2 beaten eggs. Season the sauce with salt and pepper, stir it with a whisk until it is heated through and just begins to thicken, and pour it over the sliced eggs. Sprinkle the dish with grated cheese and glaze it briefly under a hot broiler, until the top is golden but not brown. Serves four.

116

GENERAL STORE   *Genoa, Nevada*

Omelette Roger Machell

(Eggs, onion, button mushrooms, saffron, cream, parsley)

For a 6-egg omelette: In a small skillet sauté 1 small onion, thinly sliced, in 1 teaspoon of butter until it is soft and golden. Drain a 4-ounce can of button mushrooms, reserve the juice and add the mushrooms to the skillet. Sprinkle the vegetables with ½ teaspoon of flour, add a pinch of saffron and stir well. Add gradually ¼ cup of the mushroom liquor and ½ cup of heavy cream. Season sparingly with salt and pepper and simmer the sauce for 2 or 3 minutes. Make the omelette and when it is set but still soft, spread the mushrooms and part of the sauce across the center, fold it, turn it out on a platter, and pour the rest of the sauce on top. Sprinkle a band of finely minced parsley the length of the omelette and serve immediately. Serves three to four.

DAIRY FARM
in Sussex County

near Andover, New Jersey

Cheese Blintzes

(Pancake batter, cottage cheese, cream cheese, egg, lemon rind, sour cream)

Make a batter the consistency of heavy cream with 2 large eggs or 3 small ones, 1 cup of milk, 2 tablespoons of vegetable oil, 1 cup of flour and ½ teaspoon of salt. Beat the batter well. Heat ½ teaspoon of butter in a 6-inch skillet, pour in 1 tablespoon of batter and tilt the skillet in all directions so the batter will make a thin film over the entire surface. Brown the pancake on one side only and turn it out on a cloth, brown side up. Add a little butter to the pan and heat it before starting the next pancake; continue until all the batter has been used.

Cream together ¼ pound each of cottage cheese and cream cheese, 1 beaten egg, 1 tablespoon each of sugar and melted butter, the grated rind of half a lemon, and a pinch of salt. Place a heaping tablespoon of filling on each pancake, fold the left and right sides of the pancakes over their fillings and lap over the other two sides to make neatly closed bundles. Sauté the blintzes in hot butter, turning them to brown on both sides. Serve them hot with cold sour cream and a tart fruit jelly. Serves six.

BIRD'S-EYE VIEW _near Bedford, Pennsylvania_

Potato Pancakes

(Potatoes, eggs, potato flour, onion, baking powder, apple sauce)

Peel potatoes and grate them into a bowl of cold water. Drain them as soon as all are grated, put them in a clean towel and wring them dry. For each 2 cups of grated potato add 2 well-beaten eggs, 2 tablespoons of potato flour (or regular flour), 2 teaspoons of grated onion, and a pinch of baking powder. Season well with salt and pepper. Drop 4 or 5 large spoonfuls of this batter into hot fat about ⅛-inch deep in the skillet. Brown each cake well on both sides, drain them on absorbent paper and keep them hot while the rest are being cooked. Add fat sparingly to the skillet as needed and heat it well before dropping in more batter. Serve the pancakes very hot, with chilled tart apple sauce.

CHURCH STREET   *Charleston, South Carolina*

Shrimp and Oyster Bisque

(Shrimp, oysters, milk, onion, butter, cream, mace, egg yolks)

Measure out 3 cups of milk. In an electric blender, purée together 2 cups of raw oysters, with their liquor, and 1 cup of finely chopped cooked shrimp, adding a little of the milk if the mixture needs it to blend smoothly. In the top of a double boiler, sauté 1 tablespoon of grated onion in 2 tablespoons of butter until it is pale gold. Add the shellfish purée, the rest of the milk and ½ cup of heavy cream. Season the bisque with white pepper, salt to taste, and a pinch of mace, and cook it over simmering water for 30 minutes. Just before servingtime, mix a few spoonfuls of bisque with 2 beaten egg yolks. Stir this mixture gradually into the hot bisque and keep stirring until it just begins to thicken. Serve immediately with a dash of cayenne on each serving. Serves six to eight.

THE GRAND COULEE DAM   *Washington*
on the Columbia River

COLUMBIA RIVER CAVIAR IN CREAM

(Red caviar, sour cream, cream cheese, onion, black pepper)

With an egg beater mix 2 cups of sour cream with enough well-mashed cream cheese to thicken the cream somewhat. With a spoon stir in a 6-ounce jar of red salmon caviar, 1 tablespoon of grated onion, plenty of coarsely ground black pepper and a little salt to taste. Mix well, chill, and use as a spread for circles of Melba toast, or as a dip for chilled raw carrot and cucumber sticks, celery, cauliflowerets, scallions, and radishes.

121

MATHESON HAMMOCK PARK BEACH   *Miami, Florida*

GAZPACHO

(Tomatoes, crisp vegetables, garlic, herbs, consommé, oil, lime juice)

Gazpacho is a summer soup of Spanish and Cuban ancestry: Mix together 3 pounds of ripe, red tomatoes, peeled, seeded and chopped, with all their juice; 2 cucumbers, peeled, seeded and chopped; ½ cup each of minced sweet red pepper, green scallions and celery hearts; 1 clove of garlic, minced and thoroughly mashed; 2 tablespoons each of minced fresh parsley and dill; 2 cups of clear chicken consommé, and 6 tablespoons of olive oil. Season well to taste with salt, freshly ground black pepper, 3 tablespoons of fresh lime juice, and a dash of Tabasco. Chill for several hours and serve in glass bowls, with an ice cube in each bowl. Serves six to eight.

THE PRESIDENT'S MANSION
University of Alabama

Tuscaloosa, Alabama

SMOTHERED CHICKENS

(Chicken, flour, ginger, cream, butter, mushrooms)

Split 2 small broilers in halves, cut off the wing tips and soak the chickens in milk for 30 minutes. Mix together ¼ cup of flour, ½ teaspoon of salt, and ¼ teaspoon each of pepper and ground ginger. Put this in a clean paper bag, drain the chickens well, put them in the bag and shake it until they are evenly coated. Brown the chickens quickly in hot fat ¾-inch deep but do not cook them through; drain them on absorbent paper.

Sauté ½ pound of mushrooms lightly in 2 tablespoons of butter, stir in 2 cups of thin cream, season with salt and pepper, and heat just to the boiling point. Put the fried chickens in an ovenproof casserole, pour the mushrooms and cream over them and bake them covered, in a 350° oven for 35 to 40 minutes, or until the cream has thickened to a rich sauce. Serves four.

THE BROOKLYN BRIDGE *New York City*
from Dock Street, Brooklyn

CHEESE DREAM LEXY

(Bread, American cheese, chutney, curry powder, butter)

Spread two slices of bread with butter and cover them both with a thin slice of American cheese. Spread one slice with mango chutney, sprinkle lightly with curry powder, and assemble the sandwich. Sauté it slowly, first on one side, then on the other, in plenty of hot butter, and serve piping hot as soon as the cheese is melted and the bread is brown and crisp.

PIKE'S PEAK AND THE GARDEN OF THE GODS *Colorado*

BAKED BLACK BEANS

(Black beans, onion, garlic, celery, bay leaf, salt pork, rum, sour cream)

Wash 1 pound of black beans well and soak them overnight in fresh water to cover. Cook them in the same water, adding 1 more cup of water, 1 large onion, sliced, 1 whole clove of garlic, 2 stalks of celery, 1 bay leaf, several sprigs of parsley, but no salt. Simmer the beans until they are almost tender, or for about 1½ hours, then remove the garlic, celery and herbs. In a small skillet, try out 3 tablespoons of minced salt pork until the scraps are golden and add them, with the melted fat, to the beans. Then add salt, pepper and cayenne to taste, and ¼ cup of dark rum. Transfer the beans to an ovenproof casserole and if there is not enough juice almost to cover them, add a little water or consommé. Bake the beans, covered, in a 300° oven for 1 hour, stirring occasionally, until they are very tender, but not mushy, and the juice is reduced. Serve with a large sauceboat of cold sour cream. Serves six.

125

THE LINCOLN MEMORIAL   *Washington, D. C.*

Mocha Rum Souffle

(Cream, coffee, flour, butter, sugar, chocolate, rum, eggs)

Heat together ½ cup of thin cream and ¼ cup of very strong coffee. Blend 3 tablespoons of flour into 3 tablespoons of melted butter and gradually stir in the flavored cream. Add 3 tablespoons of sugar and a pinch of salt and cook the mixture over a low flame, stirring constantly, until it is smooth and thickened. Take the pan off the fire, let it cool a little and stir in gradually 4 well-beaten egg yolks. Add 2 ounces of bittersweet chocolate melted with 2 tablespoons of water and stir in 2 tablespoons of rum.

Butter a soufflé dish and dust it with fine granulated sugar. Beat 6 egg whites stiff but not dry. Fold one-third of these carefully but thoroughly into the chocolate custard, then fold in the rest lightly and pour the batter into the soufflé dish. Bake the soufflé in a preheated 350° oven for about 40 minutes, or until it is puffed high and beginning to brown. Serve immediately, with whipped cream. Serves six.

126

BUSY HARBOR   *Catalina Island, California*

CIOPPINO

(Fish, shellfish, onions, green pepper, garlic, mushrooms, tomatoes, herbs, wine)

Soak ½ cup of dried Italian mushrooms in cold water. Scrub well and steam 1 quart of clams until the shells open, and reserve the liquid. Heat ½ cup of olive oil in a large kettle, add ½ cup each of chopped onions and scallions, 1 chopped green pepper, 2 minced cloves of garlic, ¼ cup of chopped parsley, and the mushrooms, drained, and simmer all together, stirring often, for 5 minutes. Add 2½ cups of canned Italian plum tomatoes, 4 tablespoons of tomato paste, 2 cups of dry red wine, the clam liquor, 1 bay leaf, and salt and pepper. Then add 1½ pounds of sea bass (or other firm, white fish), and 1 large Dungeness crab (or 1 lobster), both cleaned and cut in pieces, and 1 pound of shelled shrimp (weighed before shelling). Cook the *cioppino,* covered and without stirring, for 15 minutes over medium heat. Then add the clams, and cook another 5 minutes. Serve in bowls, with red wine and hot French bread with garlic butter. Serves six.

127

THE FLEET   *Monterey, California*

Butterfly Shrimp

(Jumbo shrimp, fritter batter, sherry, soy sauce, garlic salt, powdered ginger)

Make a batter with 2 well-beaten egg yolks, ½ cup each of milk and sifted flour, 2 tablespoons each of salad oil and sherry, ½ teaspoon of garlic salt, and a little pepper. Let the batter rest at room temperature for 2 hours and fold 2 beaten egg whites into it just before using.

Meanwhile prepare 1 pound of raw jumbo shrimp: Cut the shells down the back with a pair of scissors. Peel off the shells but leave on the tails; then slit the shrimp half way through, down the back, with a sharp knife. Remove the black vein. Open the shrimp, lay it cut side down on a board, and flatten it by pressing hard with the heel of your hand. In a bowl mix together 1 tablespoon of soy sauce, ¼ cup of sherry and a good pinch of powdered ginger. Toss the shrimp in the mixture and let them marinate for 30 minutes. Then dip them in the batter, fry them to a golden brown in hot deep fat and drain them on absorbent paper. Serve butterfly shrimp with separate individual saucers of soy sauce and very hot mustard for dipping. Serves four.

BAYOU TECHE   *near St. Martinsville, Louisiana*

Catfish Court Bouillon

(Fish, flour, onion, garlic, herbs, tomatoes, lemon, white wine)

Catfish is the bayou fish for Louisiana court bouillon, red snapper is the best known for it, and any firm, white fish that will slice or fillet without breaking in the cooking will be good: In a large skillet heat 1 tablespoon of oil and 1 teaspoon of butter and blend in 1 tablespoon of flour. Cook this *roux* until it is golden, then add 1 onion and 2 small cloves of garlic, all minced, ½ teaspoon each of basil and thyme, 1 bay leaf, 1 tablespoon of minced parsley, salt and pepper, and a dash of Tabasco. Blend well, add 1 cup of Italian plum tomatoes and 1½ cups of water, and simmer the sauce for 20 minutes.

Cut 1½ pounds of fish fillets into serving pieces, dip them in ½ cup of white wine, season them with salt and pepper and sprinkle them lightly with flour. Arrange them side by side in the hot sauce, add the remaining white wine and half a lemon, thinly sliced. Simmer the court bouillon for 30 minutes. Remove the fish to a hot platter and discard the lemon slices and bay leaf. Pour the sauce, which should be quite thick, over the fish and serve with boiled rice. Serves three to four.

CARTER'S GROVE *near Williamsburg, Virginia*

FLAMED MUSHROOMS IN CREAM

(Mushrooms, onion, butter, brandy, sherry, heavy cream)

In a skillet simmer 2 small minced onions in 4 tablespoons of butter until they are soft. Remove the stems from 1 pound of fresh mushrooms, and wash and wipe the caps but do not peel them. Add the mushroom caps to the skillet, simmer them for 5 or 6 minutes, then add 2 tablespoons of warmed brandy, set a match to it, and shake the pan until the flame dies. Add ⅓ cup of sherry, 1 cup of heavy cream, salt and pepper to taste, and cook over a very low flame, stirring occasionally, for 25 minutes, or until the sauce has thickened. Serves three or four.

DETROIT SKYLINE   *Michigan*

Walnut Canapes

(Blue cheese, sweet butter, brandy, walnut meats, pickled onions)

Cream together ¼ pound of blue cheese and 3 tablespoons of sweet butter. Add 2 teaspoons of brandy and blend well. Spread the mixture in a smooth dome on the round sides of halved walnut meats. Press a tiny pickled onion or a caper into the top of each canapé and chill them for an hour or two before serving. This makes enough cheese spread for 4 to 5 dozen walnut halves.

THE RED BARN *Manchester, Vermont*

RED FLANNEL HASH

(Boiled potatoes, boiled beets, corned beef, onion, cream, butter)

Mix together 1½ cups each of finely diced cold boiled potatoes and beets, 1½ cups of chopped cooked corned beef, 1 medium onion, minced, ¼ cup of cream, and salt and pepper to taste. Melt 2 tablespoons of butter in an iron skillet, put in the hash and pack it down gently so that it covers the pan evenly. Cook the hash, tightly covered, over the lowest possible flame for about 35 minutes, or until a fine brown crust has formed on the bottom. Fold the hash in two as you turn it out on the platter, line up 4 poached eggs on top, and garnish with parsley. Serves four.

"TREASURE ISLAND" PIRATES' HOUSE   *Savannah, Georgia*

Asparagus and Ham in Cheese Sauce

(Ham, asparagus, cream sauce, Swiss cheese)

Use 8 large but very thin slices of baked ham and 2 dozen tender stalks of cooked asparagus. Wrap each slice of ham around 3 stalks of asparagus, and arrange the bundles side by side in a shallow buttered baking dish. Make a cream sauce with 2 tablespoons of melted butter, 1 tablespoon of flour blended in smoothly, and ½ cup each of milk and thin cream added gradually. Stir the sauce over a low flame until it is creamy, then add ½ cup of grated Swiss cheese and stir until the cheese is melted. Add salt and pepper to taste and pour this sauce over the ham rolls. Bake the dish in a 375° oven for 15 minutes, or until the top begins to glaze. Serves four.

133

SUMMER SILHOUETTES   *Cape May, New Jersey*

SALT-WATER TAFFY

(Sugar, corn syrup, cornstarch, sea water, vinegar or peppermint oil, butter)

In a large saucepan mix together 2 cups of sugar and 4 teaspoons of cornstarch. Stir in 1¼ cups of light corn syrup, 1 cup of sea water (fresh water with ½ teaspoon of salt will do), and 2 tablespoons of cider vinegar. Cook the mixture, stirring for the first 3 minutes, then without stirring at all, over medium heat. When the candy thermometer registers 256°, remove the pan from the heat and stir in 2 tablespoons of butter. Or test a drop of syrup in a glass of cold water; when it can be rolled between the fingers into a firm but not brittle ball, the candy has reached the correct "hard-ball" stage. Pour the buttered candy onto a greased platter or a marble slab and let it cool; test it by making a dent in the surface with one finger, and when the dent stays, the candy is ready to be pulled. Wet the hands with cold water, gather up the candy into a ball and pull it with the fingertips until is is white and porous. Then stretch it out into long strips, cut these into 1-inch pieces with scissors, and wrap each piece in waxed paper. Store the taffy in an airtight tin if you like it to become creamy, or leave it out if you like it hard. Instead of cider vinegar, 6 to 8 drops of peppermint oil can be added when the butter is stirred into the candy.

134

SUNLIT ANCHORAGE   *Corpus Christi, Texas*

GREEN NOODLES WITH CLAM SAUCE

(Noodles, olive oil, scallions, garlic, parsley, basil, lemon, wine, butter, clams)

In a skillet sauté 4 minced scallions, including the tender part of their green tops, in ¼ cup of olive oil until they are soft. Add 2 minced and crushed cloves of garlic, ¼ cup of minced parsley, 2 tablespoons of minced fresh basil, the grated rind of 1 lemon, freshly ground pepper, and ¼ cup of dry white wine. Simmer all together for 5 or 6 minutes until the liquid is somewhat reduced. Then add 4 tablespoons of butter and two 6-ounce cans of minced clams, preferably an Italian brand, with their juice. Stir well and simmer the sauce, covered, for 10 minutes. Boil 1½ pounds of green noodles, or spaghetti, in plenty of salted water, with 1 teaspoon of olive oil added to it, until they are tender but still firm. Drain them well, put them in a large heater casserole, and add 4 tablespoons of butter. Toss well, mix in two-thirds of the clam sauce, put the rest on top, and sprinkle with a little parsley. Cover the casserole and keep it covered until the moment of serving. Serve with broiled tomatoes. Serves six.

LIVERMORE VALLEY VINEYARDS   *near San Francisco, California*

RED WINE VENISON STEW

(Venison, brandy, herbs, onions, bacon, garlic, wine, mushrooms, sour cream)

Cut 3 pounds of tender venison into 1½-inch cubes. Marinate it for 4 to 8 hours in ¼ cup of olive oil and 1 tablespoon of brandy, adding also salt, pepper, thyme, a bay leaf, and 1 sliced onion; turn the meat several times. In a Dutch oven try out ¼ pound of bacon, finely diced, until it is lightly browned. Remove the bacon and reserve it, drain off all but 2 tablespoons of the fat and brown the venison in this. Then sprinkle the meat with 2 tablespoons of flour, blend well, and brown another 2 or 3 minutes. Add 1 whole clove of garlic and enough red wine to cover the meat, and simmer the stew, covered, for 1 hour. Then add 4 medium onions and ½ pound of mushrooms, all quartered and lightly browned in butter, the reserved bacon, the marinade, strained, and a little hot water if the sauce is already thick. Simmer the stew for another hour, or until the meat is tender. Just before serving, stir in ¼ cup of sour cream; if your venison was frozen, the blood it gave off in thawing should be combined with the cream. Serves four to six.

OLD CAPE COD INN   *Yarmouthport, Massachusetts*

CRANBERRY PIE

(Cranberries, sugar, cornstarch, salt, grated orange rind, butter, pie pastry)

Wash and pick over 1 pound of cranberries and split them in halves. Combine 2 cups of sugar, 1 tablespoon of cornstarch and ¼ teaspoon of salt, and blend this well with ½ cup of water. Stir in the cranberries and fill a 9-inch pie shell with the mixture. Sprinkle the cranberries with the grated rind of half an orange, dot them generously with butter and cover them with a lattice of pastry. Bake the pie in a 475° oven for 15 minutes, then lower the heat to 350° and bake it another 35 minutes. Serve warm or cold.

RANCH IN THE SANGRE DE CRISTO MOUNTAINS   *near Taos, New Mexico*

MEXICAN RICE

(Rice, chorizos, onion, green pepper, tomatoes, herbs, chili, peas, avocado)

In a large skillet sauté ¼ pound of sliced *chorizos*, or any highly spiced sausages, in a little olive oil until the pieces are cooked through and evenly browned. Remove the sausages and reserve them. In the fat remaining in the skillet sauté 1 medium onion and 1 green pepper, both chopped, until they are soft. Add 1 cup of raw rice, stir well, and when it begins to take on a little color, add 1 cup of hot water. Cook the rice, covered, over a low flame until the water is absorbed. Then add 1 cup of Italian plum tomatoes and 1½ cups of beef broth or tomato juice, 2 tablespoons of chopped parsley, a good pinch of orégano, salt, pepper, and 1 to 3 teaspoons of chili powder to taste. Mix well and cook the rice, still covered, for 15 minutes. Add the reserved *chorizos* and 1 cup of cooked green peas, and cook another 10 minutes, or until the liquid is absorbed and the rice is tender and fluffy. Serve Mexican rice very hot and garnished with cubes of chilled avocado. Serves four.

138

THE HERMITAGE
Home of Andrew Jackson

near Nashville, Tennessee

Narcissa Nale's Sponge Cake

(Sugar, eggs, potato flour, salt, baking powder)

Sift fine granulated sugar and measure out 1 cup. In a bowl beat 4 egg whites until they are stiff but not dry. Beat in gradually ½ cup of the sifted sugar and set aside. In another bowl beat 4 egg yolks until they are thick and lemon-colored, then beat in the other ½ cup of sugar. Measure ½ cup of sifted potato flour and sift it again, into the egg yolks, with 1 teaspoon of baking powder and ¼ teaspoon of salt. Blend well, then cut and fold the whites into the batter until it is well mixed, but do not beat it. Pour the batter into an ungreased cake pan (it should be about two-thirds full) and bake the cake in a preheated 350° oven for 30 to 40 minutes, or until the sides of the cake begin to shrink from the pan and the top is golden brown.

THE OLD TRAIN FERRY   *Ste. Geneviève, Missouri*

POTTED DUCK

(Duck, veal knuckle, white wine, vegetables, spices, brandy)

Put a 6-pound duck and a cracked veal knuckle in a kettle with 2 cups of white wine and add water to within a couple of inches of covering the duck. Add 4 green onions, 2 stalks of celery, 1 carrot, 6 cloves, 1 clove of garlic, all whole, several sprigs of parsley, 1 bay leaf and 1½ teaspoons of salt. Bring the liquid to a boil, then simmer the duck for about 2 hours, or until it is tender. Remove the duck, cool it, and store it, covered, in the refrigerator. Strain the broth, reserving the carrot, and simmer it until it is reduced to 3 cups. Cool it, and store it also in the refrigerator. Next day, or when the broth has jelled firmly, scrape off all the fat that has risen to the surface. Heat the broth to the boiling point, add 1 ounce of brandy, simmer another minute and remove from the heat. Cut the meat from the duck in large pieces, discarding all the skin and bones, and arrange them neatly in a shallow serving dish. Slice the carrot and arrange the slices on top of the duck. Pour in the broth, let the dish cool, and chill it until the broth has jelled again. Serves six.

JACKSON LAKE AND THE TETONS   *Wyoming*

Baked Ham with Apples

(Ham steak, brown sugar, dry mustard, cloves, onions, apples, butter)

Rub a 1½-inch-thick center-cut ham steak on both sides with a mixture of 2 tablespoons of brown sugar, ½ teaspoon of dry mustard and a generous grinding of black pepper. Stick 6 whole cloves around the edge of the ham slice, put it in a shallow buttered baking dish and surround it with small whole white onions, or larger ones, quartered. Add water about 1 inch deep in the dish and bake the ham, covered, for 30 minutes in a 425° oven. Then turn the ham slice over, cover it thickly with peeled, cored and sliced apples, sprinkle these with ¼ cup of brown sugar and dot them with butter. Add a little water, lower the heat to 350° and bake the ham, still covered, for 1 more hour. Baste it occasionally with the pan juices and remove the lid 10 minutes before serving to brown the apples and onions. There should be just a little thickened juice left in the bottom of the dish. Serves four to six.

141

BERKELEY ON THE JAMES RIVER   *near Richmond, Virginia*

Baking Powder Biscuits

(Flour, salt, sugar, baking powder, butter, shortening, milk)

Measure 2 cups of sifted flour and sift it again, into a bowl, with ½ teaspoon each of salt and sugar and 2 teaspoons of baking powder. With 2 knives cut in 3 tablespoons each of butter and shortening, both cold, until the mixture crumbles like meal. With a spoon mix in ½ to ⅔ cup of cold milk, a little at a time; the dough should be soft but not sticky. Put it on a floured board and knead it briefly and gently, turning it 2 or 3 times, then roll it out with a floured rolling pin. Crisp, small southern biscuits are rolled about ¼ inch thick, cut in 2-inch circles, and baked in a 425° oven for 15 minutes. Shortcake biscuits are rolled ½ inch thick, cut in 2½- or 3-inch circles, and baked in a 400° oven for 20 minutes. This recipe makes about a dozen small biscuits or 6 to 8 large ones.

THE TREE AT ROCKEFELLER PLAZA *New York City*

Roast Goose with Corn-Bread and Fruit Stuffing

(Goose, apricots, prunes, raisins, onion, parsley, corn bread, eggs)

Stuff an 8- to 10-pound goose loosely with the following stuffing: Using separate saucepans, drop ½ cup of dark seedless raisins and 1 cup each of dried apricots and prunes into boiling water to cover and steep the fruits until they just begin to plump; drain them all well. Pit the prunes and chop them coarsely; chop the raisins enough to break the skins; chop the apricots coarsely; mince enough onion and parsley to make ½ cup each; chop the raw goose liver fine; crumble enough day-old corn bread to make 3 cups; and finally, beat 2 eggs. Mix all these ingredients thoroughly, adding the eggs last. Season the dressing with salt and plenty of pepper. This is a fairly dry dressing that will acquire a moist, fluffy texture from the juices of the goose itself.

In roasting the goose, be sure to prick the skin in a number of places to release the fat. Add a little chicken stock or consommé to the pan as needed and baste the bird frequently, each time first skimming off excess fat from the pan juices. Allow 25 minutes per pound in a 325° oven.

BIRCHES IN THE ADIRONDACKS *near North Creek, New York*

MAPLE FOAMY SAUCE

(Maple syrup, egg whites, whipped cream, lemon juice)

Beat 2 egg whites stiff but not dry, and whip ½ cup of heavy cream. Dilute ¾ cup of maple syrup with 4 tablespoons of water and boil the mixture until it spins a thread, or until it registers 228° on a candy thermometer. Beat the syrup gradually into the egg whites with the egg beater. With a spoon stir in 1 teaspoon of strained lemon juice, then fold in the whipped cream. Serve with hot puddings, especially apple brown Betty (see *Index*). Serves six.

COUNTRY ESTATE
Union County

near Waverly, Kentucky

CREAM OF FRESH TOMATO SOUP WITH DILL

(Tomatoes, onion, garlic, potato starch, fresh dill, cream)

In a large saucepan sauté 1 medium onion, thinly sliced, in 1 tablespoon of melted butter until it is soft and golden. Add 1 minced clove of garlic, cook another half a minute, then add 5 ripe medium tomatoes, peeled and cut in pieces. Season the vegetables with salt, freshly ground pepper and 1 teaspoon of sugar, and simmer them gently for 10 minutes. Dissolve 1½ tablespoons of potato starch in 1½ cups of water, add this to the vegetables, and add 3 blossoms of fresh dill plant if they are available, or ¾ teaspoon of dried dill seed. Bring the soup to a boil, simmer it for 10 more minutes, then force it through a sieve. Add ¾ cup of thin cream, reheat the soup, taste it for seasoning, and serve it sprinkled with finely chopped fresh dill leaves or parsley. Serves four.

145

HOUSES ALONG THE SUSQUEHANNA
Harrisburg, Pennsylvania

FRENCH-SILK PIE

(Butter, sugar, chocolate, vanilla, eggs, pie pastry, whipped cream, almonds)

Use an electric mixer for best results. Put ¼ pound of soft butter in the small bowl of an electric mixer and beat it until it is fluffy. Add gradually ¾ cup of sugar and beat until well creamed. Add a 1-ounce square of unsweetened chocolate, first melted with a few drops of water, then a pinch of salt and 1 teaspoon of vanilla extract. When these are mixed in, add 2 eggs, one at a time, beating 3 minutes each time. Pour the chocolate cream into a baked and cooled 9-inch pastry shell, and cover it with 1 cup of heavy cream, whipped. Chill well and sprinkle with toasted chopped almonds before serving.

"French silk" may also be served in small individual ramekins, with the same topping of whipped cream and almonds. Serves six to eight.

SAN FRANCISCO BAY   *California*

MRS. BONG CHOY'S KOREAN CHICKEN

(Chicken, pineapple chunks and juice, ginger, soya sauce, garlic, oil)

A West Coast dish imported from Korea: Have a 3-pound frying chicken cut into serving pieces. Combine 1 cup of frozen or canned pineapple chunks, ¾ cup of pineapple juice, 1 tablespoon of freshly grated ginger root (or 1 teaspoon of ground ginger), 2 tablespoons of soya sauce, and 2 minced and crushed cloves of garlic. Pour this mixture over the chicken and let it marinate in the refrigerator for 4 or more hours, turning the pieces once or twice. Drain the chicken, reserving the marinade, and in a skillet brown the pieces on all sides in ¼ cup of hot oil. Remove the chicken to a casserole and discard the oil remaining in the skillet. Pour the reserved marinade over the chicken and cook it, uncovered, in a 325° oven for about 45 minutes, or until tender, basting once or twice with the juices. Serves three or four.

THE OLD VOGLER STORE   *Winston-Salem, North Carolina*

HOMINY SOUFFLE

(Hominy grits, milk, butter, eggs, bacon)

In the top of a double boiler bring to a boil 1½ cups each of milk and water. Stir in slowly ¾ cup of hominy grits, add 1 teaspoon of salt, and continue stirring until the mixture thickens. Cook it, covered, over hot water for 45 minutes, stirring occasionally, then stir in 3 tablespoons of butter and let the grits cool for 15 minutes. Beat 4 egg yolks with a pinch of white pepper until they are light and lemon colored, and stir them gradually into the grits. Beat 6 egg whites until they are stiff but not dry, and fold them carefully into the hominy mixture. Pour half this batter into a buttered soufflé dish, sprinkle over this ½ cup of very crisp finely crumbled bacon, then pour in the rest of the batter. Bake the soufflé in a preheated 350° oven for 45 minutes, or until it is well puffed and lightly browned. Serve immediately, with spiced tomatoes (see *Index*) and a tossed green salad. Serves six.

ROAD TO PYRAMID LAKE   *near Reno, Nevada*

Liptauer

(Cottage cheese, cream cheese, butter, anchovies, capers, onion, caraway, paprika)

Force ¼ pound of cottage cheese through a sieve and blend it to a smooth paste with 3 ounces of cream cheese and 4 tablespoons of soft butter. Add 3 anchovies and 1 teaspoon of capers, all finely minced, 1 tablespoon of minced onion, ½ teaspoon of caraway seeds, 1 teaspoon of Hungarian paprika, and salt and freshly ground pepper to taste. Mix well, pack the Liptauer in a small crock, and let it ripen overnight in the refrigerator. Serve with pumpernickel.

"MY OLD KENTUCKY HOME" *Bardstown, Kentucky*

CHICKEN SOUP WITH POTATO PUFFS

(Chicken broth, potatoes, eggs, shrimp, Parmesan cheese)

A festive garnish for good homemade chicken broth: Peel, boil, and mash 1 pound of potatoes, season them with salt and pepper and let them cool. Add 2 beaten eggs, blend well, and chill the mixture in the refrigerator. Roll the potato mixture into little balls no larger then a cherry. Into the center of each one press a tiny shelled shrimp of the variety that is imported in cans or found on the West Coast. Re-form the little balls, fry them in deep hot oil until they are golden, and drain them on absorbent paper. Just before servingtime, crisp them briefly in the oven. Float a few potato puffs on each serving of hot chicken soup and pass grated Parmesan cheese separately.

150

ST. MARY MISSION   *Bitterroot Valley, Montana*

CREAM CAKE

(Eggs, flour, sugar, vanilla, heavy cream, maple-syrup icing)

Let 2 eggs warm to room temperature. Sift 1½ cups of self-rising cake flour three times. Beat the eggs well, add 1 cup of sugar and ½ teaspoon of vanilla extract, and beat again. Add alternately and gradually the flour and ½ pint of heavy cream, beating after each addition. Pour the batter into a 7-by-10-inch cake pan, greased on the bottom only, and bake the cake in a 325° oven for about 40 minutes. Cool it and frost it with maple-syrup icing (see *Index*). This is one of the easiest cakes possible to make and it is invariably light and moist.

BEAR MOUNTAIN BRIDGE
on the Hudson

New York

CURRIED VEAL STEW

(Veal, bacon, onion, garlic, curry, tomato sauce, sherry, mushrooms, sour cream)

In a heavy pot melt 1½ tablespoons of butter and add 3 slices of lean bacon, diced. When the bacon begins to brown, add 1 large onion, chopped, and simmer it for 3 or 4 minutes. Add 1½ pounds of stewing veal, cut in 1½-inch cubes, and 2 cloves of garlic, minced and crushed. Brown the veal lightly on all sides, then add 1½ teaspoons of curry powder, ¾ cup of plain tomato sauce, 1 teaspoon of salt, and 1½ cups of boiling water, or enough to cover the meat well. Cover the pot and simmer the veal for 1½ hours, or until it is tender. Fifteen minutes before it is done, add ¼ cup of sherry and ¼ pound of sliced fresh mushrooms. Stir in at the last 3 tablespoons of sour cream. Serves four.

INDEPENDENCE HALL   *Philadelphia, Pennsylvania*

Lemon Chess Pie

(Lemon juice and rind, eggs, sugar, flour, corn meal, milk, butter, pie pastry)

Stir 4 lightly beaten eggs into 2 cups of sugar and add 1 tablespoon of flour mixed with 1 tablespoon of corn meal. Add gradually ¼ cup of milk, 4 tablespoons of melted butter, ¼ cup of lemon juice, and 2 teaspoons of grated lemon rind. Turn the mixture into an unbaked pie shell, and bake the pie in a 375° oven for 45 minutes. A delicious crust is formed on the surface by the corn meal.

153

THE GRAND CANYON   *Arizona*
from the South Rim

Rice Salad

(Rice, oil, vinegar, mustard, cheese, radishes, walnuts, water cress)

Cook 1 cup of rice in a large quantity of boiling salted water for 12 minutes. Drain it in a colander and let it stand over steam a few minutes to fluff. While it is still warm, add ½ cup of tart French dressing (about 5 parts oil to 2 parts vinegar, a little mustard, salt and pepper). Mix well and chill in the refrigerator. Just before serving, add ½ pound of Bel Paese or other mild cheese, cut in small dice, 10 or 12 thinly sliced radishes, 3 tablespoons of chopped walnuts, and the coarsely chopped leaves of 1 bunch of water cress. Toss well and serve with cold ham, turkey or roast beef. Serves six.

GOLD TOWN   *Central City, Colorado*

HANGTOWN FRY

(Fresh oysters, butter, eggs, cream, parsley, bacon or sausages)

The secret of this dish is to handle it lightly. Drain well 2 dozen small fresh oysters and simmer them in 2 tablespoons of melted butter for 2 or 3 minutes, or until the edges curl. Simultaneously, in another pan, start scrambling 8 eggs, first lightly beaten with 3 tablespoons of heavy cream, a little salt, and a pinch of cayenne pepper. Before the eggs are quite set, add the oysters, mix well, and turn the Hangtown Fry out on a warm platter as soon as the eggs are done but not dry. Sprinkle with parsley and serve with bacon or link sausages. Serves four.

SANTA BARBARA MISSION   *Santa Barbara, California*

Orange Cream Charlotte

(Oranges, gelatine, sugar, lemon, egg whites, cream)

Soak 1½ tablespoons of gelatine in ⅓ cup of cold water. Add it to ⅓ cup of boiling water and stir until completely dissolved. Add 1 cup of sugar, 3 tablespoons of lemon juice, and 1 cup of freshly squeezed orange juice, unstrained, but with the seeds and any coarse white pulp removed. Stir the mixture until the sugar is dissolved, then place the pan in ice water to chill. When the mixture is quite thick, beat it well with a wire whisk until it is frothy. Beat 3 egg whites stiff and whip 1 cup of heavy cream. Fold first the egg whites, then the cream into the orange-gelatine mixture. Line a dessert mold with peeled sections of orange and turn the mixture in. Or fold the orange sections into the mixture and then fill the mold. Chill the charlotte well in the refrigerator and serve it unmolded. Serves six to eight.

WHEAT FARMS   *Oklahoma*
West of Yukon

Quick Green Beans

(Young green beans, soda, salt, butter)

Wash 1 pound of tender young green beans and put them through a bean slicer. In an enamel saucepan bring 2½ quarts of water to a rapid boil. Add ½ teaspoon of soda and the beans. Bring the water back to a boil and boil them for 1½ minutes. Drain them and drop them immediately into another pot of boiling salted water. Boil them 1 minute, drain them at once, and add a large lump of butter and salt and pepper to taste. Serve immediately. Serves four to six.

MONUMENT VALLEY   *Arizona*

Stuffed Avocados

(Avocados, chicken, cucumber or celery, bacon, mayonnaise, chives, water cress)

These should be prepared very shortly before serving. Cut ripe avocados in half lengthwise, remove the pits, and sprinkle the halves with a little lemon juice, salt, and pepper. Stuff the avocados with a salad made of finely diced chicken, a little diced cucumber or celery, and 1 very crisp finely crumbled slice of bacon per serving. Dress the salad with mayonnaise, preferably homemade, thinned with a little lemon juice. Sprinkle the stuffed avocados with minced fresh chives, and serve them garnished with water cress on individual plates.

SUPREME COURT BUILDING   *Washington, D. C.*

Rock Cornish Game Birds with Mushrooms

(Rock Cornish game birds, bacon, butter, onions, chicken broth, herbs, mushrooms)

For 6 tiny Rock Cornish game birds, or 3 larger "hens," brown lightly in a Dutch oven 2 strips of diced bacon in 2 tablespoons of melted butter. Remove the bacon and reserve it, and brown 12 tiny whole onions (or 3 or 4 medium ones, quartered) in the pot. Remove the onions and reserve them also, and in the remaining fat brown the birds evenly on all sides. Discard all but about 2 tablespoons of the remaining fat, add ½ cup of chicken broth, and return the bacon and onions to the pot. Add 1 bay leaf, a pinch of thyme, and a sprig of parsley, and bake the birds, covered, in a 400° oven for 45 minutes to 1 hour, depending on their size. Fifteen minutes before they are done, add 1 cup of whole raw button mushrooms, or larger ones, sliced. Serves six.

159

MOUNT BAKER   *Washington*

Stuffed Pork Chops

(Pork chops, mincemeat, butter, chicken broth, rice, curry)

Trim the fat from 6 one-inch-thick pork chops and make a deep horizontal cut into the side of each to form a pocket. Fill each pocket with 2 tablespoons of prepared mincemeat and fasten the edges together with small skewers. In a skillet brown the chops on both sides in 2 tablespoons of hot butter. Arrange them in one layer in a baking dish, and add salt and pepper, any juice remaining in the skillet, and ¼ cup of hot water or chicken broth. Bake the chops, covered, in a 350° oven for 1 hour, removing the lid for the last 15 minutes to brown them. Serve with rice cooked in chicken broth seasoned with a little curry powder. Serves six.

FORT JEFFERSON   *Dry Tortugas, Florida*

Seedless Grapes in Cream

(Seedless grapes, sour cream, dark brown sugar)

Wash 2 pounds of seedless grapes, remove them from the stems, and dry them in a cloth. Combine the grapes with 1 pint of sour cream, putting grapes and cream in layers in a serving bowl and sprinkling, in all, 3 to 4 tablespoons of sifted dark brown sugar between the layers. Finish with a layer of cream on top and sprinkle another tablespoon of dark brown sugar over the surface. Chill in the refrigerator 6 hours or more before serving. Serves eight.

SUNLIT FAÇADE
on King Street

Charleston, South Carolina

CREAM PRALINES

(Sugar, cream, salt, vanilla, pecans)

Boil together 3 cups of sugar, 1 cup of cream, a pinch of salt, and ½ teaspoon of vanilla for about 4 minutes, or until a little of the syrup forms a soft ball when it is dropped in cold water. Stir in 3 cups of pecan meats and drop the pralines immediately by the spoonful onto waxed paper.

162

SAND DUNES
along the Columbia River

Grand Coulee Dam, Washington

DEVILLED-HAM TURNOVERS

(Devilled ham, chili sauce, pickle, flour, cream cheese, butter)

Mix together one 2¼-ounce can of devilled ham, 2 tablespoons of chili sauce and 1 tablespoon of chopped pickle. Measure 1 cup of sifted flour and cut into it one 3-ounce package of cream cheese and ¼ pound of butter. Finish blending the pastry with the fingertips, roll it out ⅛ inch thick, and cut it into circles with a biscuit cutter. Place a small spoonful of the devilled ham mixture on each circle, fold them in half and pinch the edges together. Bake the turnovers in a 400° oven for 12 to 15 minutes and serve them hot as a cocktail hors-d'oeuvre. Makes 2 dozen turnovers.

GOLD TOWN IN THE BLACK HILLS *South Dakota*

Mock Venison (Marinated Roast Leg of Lamb)

(Leg of lamb, olive oil, cider vinegar, vegetables, herbs, spices)

Wipe a leg of young lamb with a damp cloth and remove some of the fat. Marinate it for a day or more in a mixture of ½ cup of olive oil and 1 cup of mild cider vinegar, with 1 clove of garlic, 1 onion and 1 carrot, all sliced, 2 tablespoons each of chopped parsley and celery leaves, ½ teaspoon of orégano, 6 crushed peppercorns, ¼ teaspoon of powdered clove, and 1 teaspoon of salt. Turn the meat occasionally. Make a few incisions in the meat, push a sliver of garlic into each one, and spread it with a little butter. Roast the leg, uncovered, in a pre-heated 300° oven, allowing 25 minutes per pound for pink lamb, or 30 minutes for well done. Baste it occasionally with the strained marinade. When it is done, remove it to a hot platter and let it rest for 15 minutes in a warm place before carving. Meanwhile, skim as much fat as possible from the pan juices. Dilute them with a little boiling water or stock, stir in all the brown scraps, add salt to taste, simmer for a minute or two, and strain into a sauceboat.

THE GOLDEN TRIANGLE   *Pittsburgh, Pennsylvania*

JELLIED VEAL AND HAM PIE

(Veal, ham, veal knuckle, white wine, vegetables, herbs, spices, eggs, pastry)

In a soup kettle put 2 pounds of lean stewing veal cut in 1-inch cubes, 1 cracked veal knuckle, 1½ cups of dry white wine, 2 onions and 2 carrots, all sliced, 6 peppercorns, 4 cloves, 1 bay leaf, several sprigs of parsley, a pinch of thyme, and 1 teaspoon of salt. Add 2½ cups of water, or enough to cover the meat well. Bring the liquid to a boil, skim the surface, then lower the heat and simmer the meat, covered, for 1½ hours, or until it is tender. Remove the meat and discard the veal knuckle. Strain the stock, and simmer it until it is reduced to about 2½ cups. Line the bottom of a baking dish with slices of ham. Put in a layer of veal, cover with more ham, and so on until all the veal has been used, finishing with a layer of ham. Add a layer of hard-boiled eggs cut in half lengthwise. Heat the veal stock and pour in enough almost to cover the contents. Cover the dish with a circle of rich pie pastry, cut a hole the size of a dime in the center to vent the steam, and brush with 1 egg yolk mixed with 1 teaspoon of water. Bake the pie in a 450° oven for 10 minutes, reduce the heat to 350°, and bake another 15 minutes, or until the crust is light golden brown. Serve cold.

165

THE STATE CAPITOL   *Denver, Colorado*

GLORIFIED HAMBURGERS

(Ground top round, garlic, parsley, butter, Worcestershire, Italian bread)

Put ¾ pound of freshly ground top round in a bowl and sprinkle it with salt, pepper, 1 small clove of garlic, finely minced and crushed, and 1 tablespoon of minced parsley. Cut the seasonings into the meat with two knives, blending well but keeping the meat as loosely packed as when it came from the grinder. Form the mixture into two thick cakes and brown them quickly in a skillet with a little hot butter. When they are well browned on both sides, lower the flame and cook them another minute or two, or until they have begun to cook through but are still very rare in the center. Transfer them to a hot ovenproof platter and put them in a preheated 200° oven. Add 2 tablespoons of butter to the skillet, when it is melted add a good dash of Worcestershire, and when it bubbles put in two ½-inch-thick slices of Italian bread. Turn them immediately, then sauté them, turning them once more, until they are crisp and lightly browned on both sides. Put one crouton under each hamburger (these will no longer be as rare as they were), and garnish the platter with water cress and broiled tomatoes. Serves two.

166

OLD MILL   *West Milton, Ohio*

GLAZED BRUSSELS SPROUTS

(Brussels sprouts, onion, caraway, butter)

Pick over 1 quart of fresh Brussels sprouts, discard the wilted leaves, and soak the sprouts in lukewarm water for 20 minutes. Drain them, and drop them, with 1 small sliced onion and 1 teaspoon of caraway seeds, into enough lightly salted boiling water to cover. Cook them for 10 to 15 minutes, or until they are tender, and drain them well. Melt 4 tablespoons of butter in a saucepan, add the Brussels sprouts, and sauté them over low heat, shaking the pan often, until they are glazed and golden but not browned. Serves four to six.

SEASCAPE   *Yarmouthport, Massachusetts*

Oysters Poached in Butter

(Oysters, butter, shallots, white wine, pepper, toast, parsley, lemon)

Use small shucked oysters, well-drained. For ½ pint of oysters, melt 4 table-spoons of butter in a skillet and add 2 finely minced shallots. Cook the shallots for a minute or two over a low flame, then add 2 tablespoons of dry white wine, the oysters, and plenty of freshly ground pepper. Poach the oysters briefly; they are done when they begin to plump and curl around the edges. Serve on thin slices of crisp toast, with wedges of lemon and a sprinkling of parsley. Serves two.

THE QUEEN MARY AT PIER 92 *New York City*

Farewell Punch

(Strawberries, lemon juice, white wine, champagne, mint)

Hull 2 quarts of small ripe strawberries, put them in a bowl, sprinkle them with the juice of 1 lemon, and add a bottle of dry white wine (a Rhine wine or a Chablis, for instance). Chill the strawberries for several hours. To make the punch, put a good-sized block of ice in a punch bowl, add the mixture of wine and strawberries, and another bottle of white wine and 2 bottles of champagne, all well chilled. Add a few sprigs of fresh mint, stir the punch and ladle it into punch cups with a strawberry for each serving. To multiply the recipe, keep ice in reserve, and keep more strawberries marinating in wine and more white wine and champagne, unopened, in the refrigerator.

BEND IN THE ROAD   *Hurley, New York*

Sunday Eggs Sheeline

(Eggs, dry vermouth, scallions, sour cream, French bread)

With a fork beat together 8 eggs, 3 tablespoons of dry vermouth, 4 finely minced scallions, including some of their green tops, 4 tablespoons of sour cream, and salt and pepper to taste. Melt 2 tablespoons of butter in a skillet, add the eggs and scramble them over a low fire, stirring with a wire whisk, until they are creamy and light. Serve immediately on slices of toasted and buttered French bread. Serves four.

THE MISSISSIPPI NORTH OF BATON ROUGE _Louisiana_

Shrimp Jambalaya

(Shrimp, bacon fat, onions, ham, garlic, herbs, tomatoes, rice, chicken broth)

Melt 3 tablespoons of bacon fat in a flameproof casserole, and in it sauté 2 onions, chopped, and ¼ pound of ham, cut in strips. When the onion is transparent, add 1 minced and crushed clove of garlic, 1 teaspoon of orégano, 1 bay leaf, 2 cups of Italian plum tomatoes, and a little salt and pepper. Simmer the mixture for 5 minutes, then add 2 cups of raw rice and 3 cups of boiling chicken broth. Cover the casserole and simmer the jambalaya over low heat for about 5 minutes. Then add 1 pound of raw shrimp, shelled and deveined, toss rice and shrimp lightly together with two forks, and cook the jambalaya another 10 or 15 minutes, or until the rice is tender and fluffy. Add more hot broth before the cooking time is up if the mixture seems dry. Serves six.

AFTER THE SHOWER   *near Cartersville, Georgia*

POPOVERS

(Eggs, flour, salt, milk, melted butter)

In a preheated 450° oven heat well-greased iron popover pans until they are sizzling hot. Meanwhile, break 3 eggs into an electric blender, add 1 cup of flour, ¼ teaspoon of salt, and 1 cup of milk, and blend well. Stir in 1 tablespoon of melted butter and pour the batter into the hot popover pans, filling each cup not quite half way. Bake the popovers for 15 to 18 minutes at 450°, then lower the heat to 350° and bake them another 20 minutes. The longer they bake at 450° the higher they will rise, but don't push this too far or they will collapse. Serve immediately. Makes 8 to 10 popovers.

THE HEADWATERS OF THE MISSOURI *near Three Forks, Montana*

Simmered Beets

(Beets, butter, lettuce, lemon juice, chives)

Wash 8 young beets, peel them (this is no more difficult than peeling pota-toes), and shred them coarsely. Melt 6 tablespoons of butter in a heavy sauce-pan, add the beets and 2 large lettuce leaves, and mix well. Simmer the beets, covered, for 20 to 25 minutes, over the lowest possible flame, stirring occasionally. Discard the lettuce, add lemon juice, salt and pepper to taste, and serve sprinkled with chopped chives. Serves four to six.

McDONALD LAKE
Glacier National Park

Montana

Broiled Eggplant with Parsley Butter

(Eggplant, salt, pepper, vinegar, oil, butter, lemon, parsley)

Treating eggplant in this way elevates it to the level of a separate course and is sometimes called "poor man's steak."

Peel a large eggplant, cut it into slices over ½ inch thick, and cut the larger slices in half. With a sharp knife make shallow criss-cross slashes on both sides of the slices. Spread them on a platter, sprinkle them with salt, pepper, and a little vinegar, and let them stand, covered, for 3 hours. Pat the slices dry with paper toweling, brush both sides with oil, and cook them under the broiler, turning them once, until they are tender and lightly browned. Meanwhile, cream 5 tablespoons of sweet butter with the juice of ¼ of a lemon and 1 tablespoon of minced parsley. Spread the butter in the center of a warm serving dish. When the eggplant is done, arrange it over the parsley butter which will melt under the heat. Serve immediately. Serves four.

ST. PATRICK'S CATHEDRAL
from a Rockefeller Center roof garden

New York City

MINIATURE MELON AND PROSCIUTTO

(Melon balls, prosciutto or smoked ham, pepper)

Chill the necessary quantity of ripe melon balls. Shortly before servingtime, drain them well and wrap each one neatly in a small strip of Italian prosciutto or other smoked ham, sliced paper thin. Fasten each bundle securely with a toothpick, sprinkle them lightly with coarsely ground pepper, and keep them cold.

175

JOSEPHINE LAKE
Glacier National Park

Montana

SAVORY BROILED FISH

(Whole fish, thyme, oil, lemon, garlic, butter)

For any fish, fresh- or salt-water, which you wish to broil whole, the following method adds greatly to the flavor: Make shallow diagonal slashes in the skin on both sides of the fish and rub a mixture of salt, pepper, and powdered thyme into the slashes. Grill the fish over a charcoal fire, or under the broiler not too close to the flame. As it cooks, brush it frequently with oil which has been standing overnight with a slice of lemon and a crushed clove of garlic. The timing is a matter of judgment and depends on the size of the fish, but count about 15 to 18 minutes in all for a medium-sized fish and turn it after about 7 minutes. Sprinkle it with a little melted butter and lemon juice just before serving.

176

NEW ENGLAND WINTER

Pownal, Vermont

Maple-Syrup Icing

(Pure maple syrup, cream, butter)

In a deep saucepan combine 1½ cups of pure maple syrup, ¼ cup of thin cream, and 4 tablespoons of butter. Bring the mixture to a boil over moderate heat, and cook it for about 12 minutes, or until a little of the syrup forms a soft ball when dropped into cold water. Remove the pan immediately from the heat, let it cool, and beat it hard until it is barely thick enough to spread on a cake (see *Index*). Do not overcook it or it will turn to fudge before you can ice the cake.

177

THE SNAKE RIVER
below the Grand Tetons

Wyoming

CHEESE AND OLIVE TART

(Pie pastry, cheese, ripe olives, eggs, cream)

Line a 9-inch pie pan with your favorite pastry and chill it. Cover the pastry with 1 cup of grated sharp cheese and 1 cup of sliced ripe California olives. Beat 4 eggs lightly, mix them with 1 cup of thin cream, add salt, pepper, and a pinch of nutmeg, and pour this into the pie shell. Bake the tart in a 400° oven for 10 minutes, then reduce the heat to 350° and bake it for about 30 minutes, or until the custard is set and golden on top. Do not overcook. Serves six.

VIEW OVER THE BADLANDS   *South Dakota*

Scandinavian Vegetable Salad

(Green peas, carrots, beets, celery, dill, vinegar, sour cream, radishes)

An excellent salad to make in large quantities for a buffet. The following serves four: Combine 1 cup of green peas, 1 cup of diced carrots, and ½ cup of diced beets. The vegetables should first be cooked separately, in lightly salted water, until they are tender but not too soft, and drained thoroughly. Peel and dice the beets after they are cooked. Add ½ cup of finely sliced celery, 1 tablespoon of minced fresh dill (or 1 teaspoon of dried dill), 1 tablespoon of garlic wine vinegar, and salt and pepper to taste. Toss well and let the salad marinate for several hours. Shortly before serving, mix in 4 to 6 tablespoons of sour cream. Decorate the salad with a small bouquet of parsley and thinly sliced radishes.

FANEUIL HALL

Boston, Massachusetts

Boston Baked Beans

(Pea beans, salt pork, onion, molasses, brown sugar, dry mustard)

Soak 2 cups of dried pea beans in water overnight. Next day, drain the beans, cover them with fresh water, bring the water to a boil, and simmer them over low heat for about half an hour; to test, spoon out a few beans, blow on them, and if the skins burst they are ready. Meanwhile, cut ¼ pound of salt pork into ¾-inch cubes and scald these in boiling water for 2 or 3 minutes. Drain the beans and reserve the cooking water. In a 2-quart bean pot put 1 whole peeled onion (optional), half the beans and half the salt pork, drained, then the rest of the beans and pork. Push the top layer of pork down into the beans a little, and add 1 cup of the reserved bean stock heated to the boiling point and mixed with ¼ cup of molasses, 2 tablespoons of brown sugar, and 1 teaspoon each of dry mustard and salt. Add boiling water just to cover the beans, cover the pot, and bake them in a 250° oven for 6 to 8 hours without stirring them. Add a little boiling water every hour or two to keep the beans always covered with liquid. Remove the lid for the last 45 minutes of cooking (add no more water) to brown the beans on top. Serves six.

THE WHITE HOUSE   *Washington, D. C.*

Fourth-of-July Salmon

(Salmon, new potatoes, green peas, egg sauce)

In a soup kettle heat 2½ quarts of salted water with half a dozen pepper corns, several sprigs of parsley, a good pinch of thyme, and several slices of lemon. Boil the mixture for 15 minutes, then lower the heat so the liquid is barely moving. Put in a 3-pound piece of salmon wrapped in cheese cloth, and poach the fish for 25 minutes. Take the fish out of the kettle and drain it on a cloth for a minute or two. Then transfer it to a heated platter, remove the cheese cloth, and peel off the skin on the top side. Garnish the platter with steamed new potatoes, sprinkled with minced parsley, and wedges of lemon. Serve with buttered new peas and with an egg sauce which can be started shortly before the salmon has finished cooking: Blend 3 tablespoons of flour into 4 tablespoons of hot butter and add gradually ½ cup of cooking liquid from the fish kettle and 1 cup of milk. Season the sauce with salt and white pepper, simmer it, stirring often, until it is smooth and thickened, then add 2 coarsely chopped hard-boiled eggs. Serves six.

MISSION SAN ANTONIO   *San Antonio, Texas*
(The Alamo)

BARBECUED SPARERIBS

(Spareribs, red wine, tomato purée, vinegar, sugar, onion, garlic, spices)

In the refrigerator marinate for 24 hours 6 pounds of spareribs in a mixture of 1 cup of red wine, ½ cup of tomato purée, ¼ cup of tarragon vinegar, ½ cup of brown sugar or honey, 1 chopped onion, 2 peeled and split cloves of garlic, 2 tablespoons of Worcestershire, 1 tablespoon of mustard, 2 teaspoons of chili powder, 1 tablespoon of salt, a dash of Tabasco, and 2 teaspoons of orégano. Turn the meat several times.

Drain off the marinade into a saucepan and heat it but do not boil it. Arrange the spareribs on a rack in a shallow roasting pan and roast them in a 400° oven for 30 minutes. Drain off the fat in the bottom of the pan, baste the spareribs with some of the hot marinade, and repeat this process three more times, at 15-minute intervals. Then turn up the heat to 500° and roast them another 20 minutes. To barbecue the ribs out of doors, precook them in the oven for 45 minutes, then broil them over a charcoal fire, basting with the marinade, until they are brown and crisp. Serves six.

FARM IN DEUEL COUNTY   *South Dakota*

QUICK CREAMED CABBAGE

(Cabbage, milk, butter, flour, paprika)

Heat 3 cups of milk just to the boiling point, add 2 quarts of very finely shredded cabbage, and simmer them together for 2 minutes. In another saucepan, melt 4 tablespoons of butter, blend in 3 tablespoons of flour, and add gradually about ¾ cup of the hot milk from the cabbage. Blend well and add this cream sauce to the cabbage. Add salt and plenty of freshly ground pepper, and cook the cabbage, stirring often, for 3 or 4 more minutes. Sprinkle with paprika. Serves six.

FARM NEAR WINCHESTER *Virginia*

SWEET-POTATO PIE

(Sweet potatoes, eggs, brown sugar, spices, cream, butter, brandy, pie pastry)

Stir 3 lightly beaten eggs into 1½ cups of hot mashed sweet potatoes. Add ⅓ cup of brown sugar, a pinch of salt, ¼ teaspoon each of cinnamon, allspice, and ginger, ¼ cup of light cream, 2 tablespoons of melted butter, and 2 tablespoons of brandy. Mix well and beat the mixture for about a minute. Turn it into an unbaked pie shell, and bake the pie in a 450° oven for 10 minutes. Reduce the heat to 350° and bake another 30 minutes, or until the filling is set and the crust is golden brown.

ROADSIDE BARN

Foster, Rhode Island

Roast Leg of Lamb with Mint Sauce

(Leg of lamb, and a sauce of cider vinegar, sugar, salt, fresh mint, jelly)

Remove the fell and some of the fat from a 6- to 8-pound leg of young lamb if you wish, wipe the meat with a damp cloth, and roast it, fat side up and uncovered, in a preheated 300° oven. The roasting time is of course a matter of taste. Allow 18 minutes per pound for medium pink, or 25 to 30 minutes for well done. Serve with mint sauce:

Boil together for 3 or 4 minutes 1 cup of cider vinegar, ¼ cup of water, 4 scant tablespoons of granulated sugar, and ½ teaspoon of salt. Pour the syrup over ⅓ cup of finely chopped fresh mint leaves, cover, and let the sauce infuse for at least 1 hour. Chill it, and just before serving add ½ cup of apple or mint jelly. Mix together with a fork just enough to break the jelly into small pieces. Serves six to eight.

VINEYARDS NEAR CUCAMONGA   *California*
San Bernardino County

CALIFORNIA COQ AU VIN

(Chicken, green pepper, onions, raisins, olives, olive oil, tomatoes, red wine, orégano)

Have two 3-pound chickens cut into serving pieces. Roll the pieces in flour seasoned with salt, pepper, and monosodium glutamate. Arrange them in layers in a large casserole, with the legs and less meaty pieces in the bottom and the breast pieces over them. Spread some of the following mixture between each layer and over the top: Combine 1 green pepper, chopped, 2 medium onions, thinly sliced, ½ cup of seedless raisins, one 4½-ounce can of chopped olives, ⅓ cup of olive oil, 1 cup of peeled and coarsely chopped tomatoes, 1½ to 2 cups of red wine, and ½ teaspoon each of salt and orégano. Bake the chicken, uncovered, in a 300° oven for about 2½ hours, or until the sauce is reduced and thickened. Serve with rice cooked in chicken consommé. Serves eight.

186

THE BEACH AT SAN FRANCISCO   *California*

Hawaiian Ambrosia

(Oranges, pineapple, coconut, ginger)

Combine 2 cups of peeled orange sections, 1 cup of fresh pineapple cubes, 1 cup of shredded coconut (preferably fresh), 1 cup of orange juice, 2 teaspoons of grated orange rind, and 1 teaspoon of finely minced preserved or candied ginger. Chill well. Serves six.

THE SCHUYLKILL RIVER
from the Aquarium

Philadelphia, Pennsylvania

Curried Chicken in Cream

(Chicken, butter, vegetables, apple, curry powder, chicken broth, cream, almonds)

In a large skillet sauté a small roasting chicken, cut in serving pieces, in 2 tablespoons of butter until the pieces are brown on all sides. In another skillet sauté 1 onion, 1 carrot, 1 stalk of celery, ½ green pepper, and 1 tart apple, all finely chopped, in 3 tablespoons of butter until they begin to soften. Sprinkle the vegetables with 1 to 2 tablespoons of curry powder, or more, depending on your taste for curry, and blend well. Add 1½ cups of hot chicken broth and pour this mixture over the browned chicken. Cover the skillet and simmer the chicken for 25 minutes, or until it is tender, then remove the pieces to a serving dish and keep them hot. Blend a little of the liquid in the skillet with 1½ tablespoons of flour, return it to the pan, add 1 cup of heavy cream, and salt to taste, and thicken the sauce over low heat, stirring constantly. Strain it over the chicken and sprinkle it with chopped blanched almonds. Serve with rice and chutney. Serves four.

188

THE CITY HALL   *San Francisco, California*

Rumaki

(Chicken livers, water chestnuts, bacon)

For each rumaki, wrap together in half a strip of bacon a piece of raw chicken liver and half a canned water chestnut. Pin each roll securely through the center with a wooden toothpick. Arrange the rumakis on a cake rack in a shallow pan and bake them in a 400° oven until the bacon is brown and crisp.

BRYCE CANYON

Utah

Cheese Ramekins

(Swiss cheese, toast, eggs, cream)

Butter 6 individual baking dishes, put a piece of fresh toast, trimmed and buttered, in the bottom of each one, and fill them three-quarters full with the following batter: Beat together 4 egg yolks and 1½ cups of cream, stir in 1½ cups of grated Swiss cheese, add salt to taste and a speck of cayenne, and fold in 4 stiffly beaten egg whites. Bake in a 375° oven for 30 minutes and serve immediately. Serves six.

THE LIGHTHOUSE   *Cape Elizabeth, Maine*

CLAM AND TOMATO BOUILLON

(Clam broth or juice, mixed-vegetable juice, butter, dill, whipped cream)

Heat together equal parts of canned tomato-and-mixed-vegetable juice and clam broth or bottled clam juice, adding 1½ teaspoons of butter for each cup of liquid. Serve garnished with minced fresh dill and a generous spoonful of lightly salted whipped cream.

191

OLD WATER MILL   *near Gauley Bridge, West Virginia*

Susan Rockey's Corn-Meal Batter Cakes

(Yellow corn meal, baking soda, egg, buttermilk)

    Sift together 1 cup of yellow corn meal, ½ teaspoon of baking soda and ½ teaspoon of salt. Stir in 1 beaten egg and 1¼ cups of buttermilk, and beat the batter with a wooden spoon until it is smooth. Dip it by spoonfuls onto a hot griddle or iron skillet greased with butter or bacon fat. Let the cakes brown on one side and turn them once to brown on the other. Remove them to a hot platter and add a very little fat to the griddle before starting the next cakes. Makes 10 to 12 cakes.

THE CHESAPEAKE BAY BRIDGE *Maryland*

Baltimore Crab Cakes

(Crab meat, eggs, onion, dry mustard, Worcestershire, mayonnaise, parsley, crumbs)

Mix together 1 pound of cooked crab meat, 1 egg, 2 teaspoons of minced onion, 1 teaspoon of dry mustard, 1 teaspoon of Worcestershire, 1 tablespoon of mayonnaise, and 2 tablespoons of chopped parsley. Add salt and freshly ground pepper and chill the mixture for an hour or two. Form the crab meat into 4 cakes, pressing the meat firmly together. Dip the cakes in seasoned flour, then in beaten egg, then in bread crumbs. In a skillet sauté them quickly in 2 tablespoons of hot butter, turning them once, until they are brown on both sides. Serve them with coleslaw and wedges of lemon, or with a tartar sauce spiced with horseradish. Serves four.

LITTLE NECK BAY   *New York*
Long Island

Picnic Roast Clams

(Hard-shell clams, butter, lemon juice, garlic)

These can be made at home in a 450° oven, but they are more fun and some-how taste best on the beach, roasted over a charcoal fire. Hard-shell clams are best. Place the clams on a grate over a bed of glowing coals; they are done in about 3 minutes, or when the shells are well opened by the heat. Very large clams may need an extra 30 seconds of cooking to be heated through. Do not overcook, however, as the clams will toughen, and be sure to discard any that refuse to open. Keep hot on a corner of the fire a saucepan of butter sauce for dipping the clams. The proportions are the juice of half a lemon, squeezed in to taste, to each ½ pound of butter. Add 2 large cloves of garlic, peeled and cut in half, and let them steep in the hot butter for 15 minutes before using the sauce. Then remove them or not, as you wish. The only serving utensils necessary are tongs for taking the clams from the fire and quantities of paper napkins.

THE STERNWHEELER "SWANEE"   *Dearborn, Michigan*

Chicken Tetrazzini

(Chicken, mushrooms, spaghetti, butter, chicken broth, cream, sherry, Parmesan)

Simmer a young chicken in salted water just to cover until it is tender. Cool it in the cooking liquid, then remove all the meat, cut it in strips, and return the skin and bones to the cooking liquid. Simmer the broth until it is reduced to about 2 cups. Sauté ½ pound of sliced mushrooms in a little butter until they are soft and the liquid has evaporated, and boil ½ pound of spaghetti in salted water until it is just tender. Make a sauce with 2 tablespoons of flour blended into 3 tablespoons of melted butter and 2 cups of the chicken broth, strained and skimmed, added gradually. Stir the sauce over medium heat until it is slightly thickened, then add 1 cup of warm cream and 3 tablespoons of sherry. Combine the hot cooked spaghetti, the mushrooms, and half the sauce; put the mixture in a buttered baking dish and make a "well" in the center. Into this put the chicken meat mixed with the rest of the sauce. Sprinkle with grated Parmesan and bake in a moderate oven until the top is lightly browned. Serves six.

195

CASEY FARM   *North Kingston, Rhode Island*

BREAD AND CHEESE CHARLOTTE

(Bread, butter, sharp cheese, eggs, milk, pepper, mustard)

Trim the crust from slices of good white bread, butter the slices, and cut enough of them into oblong strips to line the inside of a 1½-quart baking dish. Line only the sides, not the bottom, and place the pieces buttered side against the dish. Trim and butter more slices and cut them into ½ inch squares, using enough to make about 3½ cups. Grate enough old-fashioned store cheese or sharp Cheddar to make 1 cup. Starting with bread, arrange the diced bread and grated cheese in layers in the baking dish, grinding a little pepper over each layer of bread. Beat 2 eggs, add 1 cup of milk and ½ teaspoon each of salt and dry mustard, and mix well. Pour this over the bread and cheese, and arrange more buttered slices of bread, quartered into triangles and buttered side up, in a circle on the top of the "charlotte." Let the dish rest for 20 minutes before baking it in a 350° oven for 30 minutes, or until it is puffy and golden brown. Serves four to six.

THE SAN FRANCISCO PEAKS   *Arizona*

Paprika Turkey

(Turkey meat, onion, butter, paprika, stock, cream, sherry, egg yolks, noodles)

Sauté 2 tablespoons of minced onion in 2 tablespoons of melted butter until the onion is golden. Add 1½ tablespoons of Hungarian paprika, blend well, and add ½ cup each of turkey stock and light cream, and salt and pepper. Simmer the sauce, stirring often, for 5 minutes. Add 2 cups of cooked turkey meat cut in large dice, and cook the mixture over low heat until the turkey is hot. Then add 2 egg yolks mixed with another ½ cup of cream and 2 tablespoons of sherry, and continue cooking, stirring constantly, without letting the sauce boil, until it thickens. Serve with noodles sprinkled with bread crumbs that have been sautéed in a little butter until they are golden brown and crisp. Serves four.

197

HARVARD HALL   *Cambridge, Massachusetts*

Aunt Polly's Rice Bread

(Rice, flour, butter, shortening, salt, baking powder)

Cream together well ½ cup of sugar and 4 tablespoons each of butter and vegetable shortening. Sift together 1 cup of flour, 2 teaspoons of salt, and 2 teaspoons of baking powder. Combine the shortening-sugar mixture, the flour, and 1 cup of boiled rice. Add 2 beaten eggs and 1 cup of milk, and pour the batter in a thin layer into a rectangular buttered baking pan. Bake the rice bread in a 400° oven for about 15 minutes. When it is browned, cut it in squares and serve it hot, with butter.

198

OLD MINING TOWN   *Tombstone, Arizona*

ICED CUCUMBER SOUP

(Cucumbers, scallions, tarragon, cream, chicken broth, egg yolks, lemon, sour cream)

In a saucepan melt 2 tablespoons of butter and add 2 medium cucumbers, washed and diced but not peeled, and 2 sliced scallions, including a little of their green tops. Simmer the vegetables, covered, over a low fire until they are soft but not browned. Add salt, pepper, ½ teaspoon of chopped fresh tarragon (or ¼ teaspoon dried tarragon), and 1 cup of light cream. Simmer the mixture for 5 minutes, then purée it in an electric blender, and combine it with 3 cups of clear chicken broth. Heat the soup, add 2 lightly beaten egg yolks first mixed with a few spoonfuls of the soup, and stir until it just begins to thicken. Do not let it boil. Pour the soup into a cold container, let it cool, then chill it in the refrigerator. Serve in chilled bowls; float a thin slice of lemon in each bowl and drop a spoonful of sour cream on the lemon. Serves six.

PIER AT ROCKLAND *Maine*

Broiled Scallops

(Scallops, oil, white wine, lemon juice, garlic, thyme)

Wash 1 pound of sea scallops, drain and dry them well, and cut them in halves or quarters. Marinate the scallops for an hour or more in a mixture of ½ cup of salad oil, ¼ cup of white wine, 1 tablespoon of lemon juice, 1 minced and crushed clove of garlic, a good pinch of thyme, and a little salt and freshly ground pepper. Pour off the marinade and spread the scallops in a shallow pan. Broil them under a high flame for about 5 minutes, basting once or twice with some of the marinade and turning them once to cook them evenly. Serve immediately on toothpicks as a cocktail hors-d'oeuvre. Or serve them with strips of crisp bacon as a main course for three.

MIDTOWN SILHOUETTES   *New York City*

Grand Central Oyster Stew

(Fresh oysters, oyster or clam liquor, butter, milk, cream, seasonings)

Remove 2½ dozen freshly opened oysters from their shells. Save the liquor and measure out 2 cups (or use 2 cups of clam liquor or juice). In a saucepan heat 4 tablespoons of butter with a little celery salt, paprika and Worcestershire. When the butter bubbles, add the oysters and oyster liquor, and simmer them for 2 or 3 minutes, or until the edges begin to curl. Add 1 pint each of milk and thin cream, bring the soup to a boil and serve immediately. Top each serving with a small piece of butter and a dash of paprika. Serves four.

THE FISH HOUSE
Calderwoods

Vinal Haven, Maine

Baked Flounder with Minced Clams

(Flounder fillets, white wine, onion, butter, cream, minced clams)

Arrange 1½ pounds of fillets of flounder or sole in a shallow baking dish, add 1 small onion, finely minced, and 1 cup of dry white wine, and bake the fillets in a preheated 325° oven until they are just done, or for 15 to 20 minutes. Transfer the fillets carefully to a heatproof serving dish and keep them warm. Make a sauce with 1½ tablespoons of flour blended into 2 tablespoons of melted butter and 1 cup of the hot cooking liquid added gradually. Simmer the sauce, stirring often, until it is smooth and thickened, then add ½ cup of heavy cream and one 8-ounce can of minced clams, drained. Taste the sauce for seasoning, stir it until it is hot but not boiling, and pour it over the fish fillets. Put the dish under the broiler for a few minutes until the sauce bubbles and begins to glaze. Serves four.

202

OLD STURBRIDGE VILLAGE *Sturbridge, Massachusetts*

Open Maple Apple Pie

(Apples, maple sugar, cinnamon, butter, heavy cream, pie pastry)

Line a 9-inch pan with your favorite pie pastry. Pare and core 4 tart apples, slice them, and arrange them in the pastry shell. Sprinkle the apples generously with maple sugar, add a little cinnamon, and dot them with butter. Pour over them ⅔ cup of heavy cream. Bake the pie in a 450° oven for 10 minutes, then lower the heat to 350° and continue baking until the apples are well softened.

GHOST FAÇADE   *Silver City, New Mexico*

Roast Chicken with Spiced Rice Stuffing

(Chicken, rice, stock, onion, mushrooms, celery, herbs, spices)

Prepare a stuffing for a 4- to 5-pound roasting chicken as follows: Stir ⅔ cup of washed, uncooked rice into 2 tablespoons of melted butter and cook it, stirring, over a low fire, until the grains are golden. Add 1¾ cups of hot chicken stock, cover the saucepan, and cook the rice slowly for about 15 minutes, or until it is cooked but still firm. In 1½ tablespoons of melted butter sauté for 3 minutes 1 small minced onion and ¼ pound of fresh sliced mushrooms. Add ¾ cup of finely diced celery, and cook all together for 3 more minutes. Mix together the sautéed vegetables, the cooked rice, and the outer rind of 2 small oranges, finely grated, 1 tablespoon of minced parsley, ½ teaspoon of ground ginger, a dash of pepper, 1 tablespoon of soya sauce, and a little salt to taste. Stuff the chicken loosely, sew up the cavity, truss the bird, and place it on a rack in a roasting pan. Roast it for about 2 hours in a 325° oven. Warm together in a small saucepan ¼ cup of water, 1 tablespoon of vinegar, 1 tablespoon of honey, and 1¼ tablespoons of soya sauce. Baste the chicken often with the pan juices, adding each time a spoonful of this mixture. Serves four.

MISSION DOLORES *San Francisco, California*

Ginger-Ale Julep

(Fresh mint, sugar, ice, ginger ale)

In a saucepan crush 1 cup of fresh mint leaves (quite well packed) with 1 cup of sugar. Add ½ cup of water and boil the mixture, stirring, for 7 minutes. Strain the syrup, add a drop or two of green food coloring, and let it cool. To serve, half fill tall glasses with crushed ice, add 2 tablespoons of the mint syrup, and fill the glasses with chilled ginger ale. Garnish with fresh mint.

GAY HEAD
Martha's Vineyard, Massachusetts

Curried Lobster in Cream

(Lobster meat, butter, chives, sherry, curry powder, cream)

In a skillet over a low fire heat 4 cups of cooked sliced lobster meat in 4 tablespoons of melted butter just until the lobster is pale gold. Add 1 tablespoon of minced fresh chives and 3 tablespoons of dry sherry, and blend well. Blend 2 teaspoons of curry powder with a little heavy cream, add enough cream to make 2 cups, and pour this over the lobster. Add salt to taste, and simmer all together for about 3 minutes. Serve immediately, with rice or on toast. Serves six to eight.

BRANDON ON THE JAMES
Prince George County

Virginia

Baked Country-Cured Ham

(Ham, brown sugar, cloves, allspice, bay leaves, cider, crumbs, mustard, vinegar)

Wash and scrub well a country-cured ham. Soak it in water to cover for 24 hours. Drain and rinse it, cover it with fresh water, and add ½ cup of brown sugar, 12 whole cloves, 6 whole allspice, 4 bay leaves, and 2 cups of cider. Cover the kettle, bring the liquid slowly to a boil, and simmer the ham for 20 to 25 minutes per pound, keeping the liquid just below the boiling point at all times. Let the ham cool completely in the cooking liquid, then remove it, take off the skin, and trim off some of the fat. Mix together ¾ cup of brown sugar, ½ cup of fine bread crumbs, and 2 teaspoons of dry mustard, and add enough cider vinegar, about 3 tablespoons, to bind the mixture together. Spread this over the fat side of the ham, and with a sharp knife score the surface with criss-crossing diagonal slashes; push a whole clove into each diamond of the criss-cross pattern. Bake the ham in a preheated 425° oven for 20 minutes, then lower the heat to 350° and bake the ham for another 30 minutes.

19TH-CENTURY SHOP FRONT   *Providence, Rhode Island*

Brunch Muffins with Ham

(Bran cereal, milk, egg, butter, flour, baking soda, parsley, onion, ham)

Soak ½ cup of bran cereal in ¾ cup of milk. Add 1 beaten egg and 2 table-spoons of melted butter. Sift together 1 cup of self-rising flour, 1 teaspoon of baking soda, ½ teaspoon of salt, and ¼ teaspoon of pepper. To the flour add 1 tablespoon of minced parsley, 1 teaspoon of minced onion, and 2 cups (measured loosely) of ground cooked ham. Combine the two mixtures lightly and quickly. Partly fill greased muffin tins with the batter, and bake the muffins in a 375° oven for about 20 minutes.

WINTER DRYDOCK   *Portsmouth, New Hampshire*

Roast Pheasant with Bread Sauce

(Pheasant, pan gravy, and a sauce of milk, seasonings, bread crumbs, cream, butter)

Roast a pheasant according to a good standard recipe, basting it often, and serve the pan juices, diluted with a little hot chicken broth and skimmed of fat, in a sauceboat. Serve also, in another sauceboat, the traditional bread sauce of English origin for feathered game and poultry: In the top of a double boiler put 1½ cups of hot milk, half a bay leaf, and 1 medium onion stuck with 6 or 8 cloves. Let the milk and seasonings infuse over simmering water for 20 minutes. Remove the onion and bay leaf, put the pan over direct heat, and stir in 1 generous cup of soft white bread crumbs. Simmer the mixture for 3 or 4 minutes, stirring often, then put the pan back over simmering water for 10 minutes. Add 1 tablespoon each of butter and cream, salt and pepper to taste, and a dash of cayenne. Brown ½ cup of coarse bread crumbs in 2 tablespoons of melted butter and serve them in a separate bowl to sprinkle over the bread sauce. Serves four to six.

DALLAS SKYLINE   *Texas*

Cocktail Frankfurters in Wine

(Miniature frankfurters, butter, white wine, rosemary)

For a party of 10 to 12 people: Melt 1 teaspoon of butter in a large skillet, add 1½ pounds of small cocktail frankfurters, and sauté them gently until they are heated through and just beginning to brown. Do not overcook them. Transfer the frankfurters to a heated casserole and add 2 tablespoons of butter, ¼ cup of dry white wine, and a good pinch of rosemary. Put the casserole, covered, in a very slow oven, 200° or less. Serve the frankfurters as needed, a dozen or so at a time, on toothpicks and with mustard, keeping the remainder warm in the oven. The frankfurters will stay ready to serve at a moment's notice without overcooking for about 1½ hours.

MORMON TEMPLE
and the State Capitol

Salt Lake City, Utah

VEAL CHOPS IN SOUR CREAM

(Loin veal chops, butter, mushrooms, basil, dry vermouth, sour cream)

In a skillet, over high heat, brown 4 thick loin veal chops well on both sides in 2 tablespoons of hot butter. If they give off very much liquid, pour it off, add more butter to the pan, and continue browning the chops. Then lower the heat, cover the skillet, and simmer them for 20 to 25 minutes. Turn them once and add butter sparingly if they tend to stick. Meanwhile, sauté ½ pound of fresh mushrooms, sliced, in 1 tablespoon of butter. Season them with salt, pepper, and a generous pinch of basil, and when all their liquid has evaporated add ¼ cup of dry vermouth. Simmer for about 1 minute, and add 1 cup of sour cream. Blend well and heat the sauce, stirring constantly, without letting it boil. Transfer the chops to a heated platter, stir any juices left in the skillet into the sauce, taste for seasoning, and pour it over the chops. Serve with rice. The same dish may be made with chicken breasts. Serves four.

LOOKOUT POINT AT THE FONTANA DAM   *near Knoxville, Tennessee*
in the Great Smoky Mountains

Spiced Tomatoes Alvin Kerr

(Tomatoes, onion, butter, brown sugar, paprika, cloves, cinnamon, bay leaf)

Peel 6 firm medium tomatoes, leaving the stem ends intact. In a skillet sauté ½ onion, minced, in 4 tablespoons of butter until it is soft. Add 3 tablespoons of brown sugar, ¼ teaspoon of paprika, 4 cloves, a ½-inch length of stick cinnamon, finely crumbled, 1 bay leaf, freshly ground pepper, and salt, and blend well. Put the tomatoes in the skillet, stem ends down, and simmer them, uncovered, over a very low flame for 1 hour. Baste them occasionally with the pan juices, but do not stir or break them. Serves four to six.

GEORGIAN HOUSE IN NEWCASTLE   *Delaware*

Oatmeal Bread

(Flour, rolled oats, molasses, butter, salt, sugar, water, yeast)

In a large bowl mix together ¼ cup of molasses, 2 tablespoons of butter, 1 teaspoon of salt, 1 tablespoon of sugar, and 3 cups of boiling water. When the butter has melted completely, add 2½ cups of regular rolled oats (*not* the quick-cooking kind), and mix well. When the mixture has cooled to lukewarm, add 1 cake of yeast dissolved in ½ cup of lukewarm water, and 6 cups of sifted flour. Beat the dough until it is smooth and let it rise in a warm place, covered, until it doubles in bulk. Punch it down, knead it well on a lightly floured board, and let it rise in a greased bowl until it doubles in bulk again. Punch down and knead the dough a second time, shape it into 2 loaves and put them in greased bread pans. Let them rise a third time, for 1 hour, and bake them in a 400° oven for 40 to 50 minutes. Cool the loaves on wire racks.

213

MISPILLION LIGHT
near Milford

Delaware

Golden-Fried Shad Roe

(Shad roe, lemon, crumbs, egg, sweet butter, oil, water cress)

Parboil shad roe very slowly in enough water to cover, adding salt and 1 table-spoon of vinegar. After about 12 minutes, or when the roe is firm, drain it, cover it with cold water and let it stand for 5 minutes. Drain and dry it thoroughly, and cut it into ¾-inch sections. Dip these in lemon juice, then in fine crumbs, in beaten egg, and again in crumbs. Fry the roe in sweet butter and oil combined, about ⅜ inch deep, in a frying pan. When the roe is golden on each side, place it on a hot platter and garnish it with lemon wedges and fresh water cress. Serve with creamed potatoes.

SNOW SCENE   *Chester, Vermont*

Peppermint-Stick Ice Cream

(Peppermint-stick candy, milk, heavy cream, bittersweet chocolate)

Crush ½ pound of peppermint-stick candy and soak it overnight in 2 cups of milk. Set the refrigerator controls at "very cold." Whip 1 pint of heavy cream and fold it into the peppermint mixture. Put the cream into a deep refrigerator ice tray. If the tray has no fitted lid, smooth a large piece of aluminum foil over the surface of the cream and fold the edges securely under the tray. Freeze the ice cream for 2 to 4 hours, or until it is firm. Serve sprinkled with grated bittersweet chocolate.

THE FLAG HOUSE   *Baltimore, Maryland*

KIDNEY STEW

(Veal kidneys, onion, butter, beef broth, bay leaf, sherry, parsley)

First remove all the fat and skin from 2 veal kidneys, split them, and cut out the hard center membranes with scissors. Then wash them under running water, slice them thinly, and toss the slices in a bowl with 1 tablespoon of vinegar. In a skillet sauté 1 small minced onion in 3 tablespoons of butter until it is soft. Dry the sliced kidneys in a towel, add them to the skillet, and cook them over a brisk flame for about 4 minutes, stirring often. Remove the kidneys to a hot plate. Add 1 teaspoon of butter to the pan juices, lower the heat, and blend in 1 scant tablespoon of flour. Add gradually 1 cup of beef broth and 1 bay leaf, and simmer the sauce, stirring occasionally, for 5 or 6 minutes, or until it thickens. Return the kidneys to the skillet, with any juice that has drained from them, and reheat them over a low flame for 2 minutes. Add 2 tablespoons of dry sherry, remove the bay leaf, and serve the kidneys in a rice ring or with buttered noodles, and with a sprinkling of chopped parsley. Serves four.

216

MENUS

Menus

BRUNCHES

Hominy soufflé, 148
Spiced tomatoes Alvin Kerr, 212
Vermont baked apples, 17
Coffee

Screwdrivers

Sunday eggs Sheeline, 170
Green salad Caroline, 97
Camembert
French bread
Fresh cherries and apricots

Homemade sausage-meat patties, 36
Buttered hominy grits
Fried apple rings
Popovers, 172 Coffee

Bloody Marys

Shirred eggs with caper sauce, 20
Tossed green salad, French dressing
Baking powder biscuits, 142
Raspberries and whipped cream
cheese, 68

BARBECUES

Rumaki, 189
Rock salt barbecued steak, 37
Colache, 99
French bread
Monterey Jack cheese
Hawaiian Ambrosia, 187
Coffee
California Pinot Noir

Cheddar dollars, 6
Barbecued spareribs, 182
Hot potato salad, 18
Sliced cucumbers and water cress
with French dressing
Cheese cake, 35
Iced coffee

Rosé wine

BEACH PICNIC

Stuffed eggs
Picnic roast clams, 194
Baked country-cured ham, 207
Rice salad, 154
Fresh fruit
Coffee

Chilean Riesling

PARTY LUNCHEONS

Jellied madrilène
Ham à la King, 79
Asparagus, drawn butter
Lemon chess pie, 153

Minced veal in cream, 64
Steamed rice
Sliced cucumber salad, French dressing
Apple brown Betty, 85

Omelette Roger Machell, 117
Tossed green salad, French dressing
Wisconsin Brie   French rolls
Tropical ice, 82
Demitasse

California Riesling

Iced cucumber soup, 199
Broiled scallops, 200
Pineapple sherbet
Chinese almond cakes, 49
Demitasse

California Pinot Blanc

Baltimore crab cakes, 193
Cole slaw, 105
Aunt Polly's rice bread, 198
Sliced peaches
Iced tea

Daiquiris   *Cheddar dollars, 6*

Gazpacho, 122
Broiled King crab legs, 73
Lemon sponge, 46
Demitasse

Chilean Riesling

Dry Sherry *Crackers and Liptauer, 149*

Chilled poached trout, 90
Hot French bread   Sweet butter
Chocolate icebox mousse, 19
Lady fingers

California Folle Blanche

Stuffed avocadoes, 158
Open blueberry pie, 26
Iced coffee

Clam and tomato bouillon, 191
Asparagus and ham in cheese sauce, 133
Lemon sponge, 46

SUPPERS FOR TWO

Oysters poached in butter, 168
Green salad Caroline, 97
Philadelphia peach ice cream, 55
Chinese almond cakes, 49

California Pinot Blanc

Glorified hamburgers, 166
Broiled tomatoes
French bread   Langlois blue cheese
Ripe pears

California Pinot Noir

FAMILY DINNERS

Baked ham with apples, 141
Mashed potatoes
Boiled white onions in butter
Indian pudding, 54

Savory broiled fish, 176
Steamed new potatoes
Quick green beans, 157
Open maple apple pie, 203

Veal chops in sour cream, 211
Buttered noodles
New peas
Vermont baked apples, 17

Clam and tomato bouillon, 191
Planked Lake Michigan whitefish, 8
Broccoli
Open blueberry pie, 26

Mint-barbecued lamb, 104
Kasha (plain), 106
Simmered beets, 173
Seedless grapes in cream, 161

Mock venison, 164
Steamed potatoes
Asparagus, drawn butter
Filbert pudding, 69

Broiled rib lamb chops
Sour cream and chives
baked potatoes, 10
Quick green beans, 157
Lemon sherbet
Narcissa Nale's sponge cake, 139

Boiled beef, horseradish sauce, 47
Boiled potatoes
Glazed Brussels sprouts, 167
Sliced tomato salad
Rhubarb crumble, 114

Steak Barry Wall, 59
Broiled onions, 4
French-fried potatoes
Quick green beans, 157
Orange cream charlotte, 156

221

TO FEED A CROWD

Cocktail frankfurters in wine, 210
Spite House fish chowder, 62
Tossed green salad, French dressing
Toasted pilot crackers
Aged Cheddar cheese
Pumpkin ice cream cake, 113
Coffee

Chilean Riesling

Green noodles with clam sauce, 135
Broiled tomatoes
Escarole salad, French dressing
Italian bread sticks
Assorted cheeses
Fruit
Espresso coffee

White Chianti

PARTY DINNERS

Oysters poulette, 100
Potted duck, 140
Steamed rice
Field lettuce salad, French dressing
Filbert pudding, 69
Café brûlot, 102

Imported white and red Bordeaux

Vichyssoise, 34
Roast pheasant, 24
Steamed wild rice
Endive and water cress salad
Mocha rum soufflé, 126
Demitasse

Imported red Bordeaux

Cherrystone clams on the half shell
Fourth of July salmon, 181
New potatoes
Green peas
Open blueberry pie, 26
Coffee

New York State Elvira

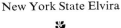

Rumaki
Mrs. Bong Choy's Korean chicken, 147
Kasha (plain), 106
Sliced avocado and water cress
with French dressing
Tropical ice, 82
Demitasse

California Pinot Chardonnay

Butterfly shrimp, 128
Steamed rice
Chinese spinach, 91
Vanilla ice cream
with preserved kumquats
Chinese almond cakes, 49
Tea or Coffee

California Folle Blanche

BUFFETS

Baked country-cured ham, 207
Batter bread, 43
Buffet party cole slaw, 105
Spiced tomatoes Alvin Kerr, 212
Baking powder biscuits, 142
Sweet-potato pie, 184   Ambrosia, 109
Coffee

California Sauvignon Blanc

Jellied veal and ham pie, 165
Hot potato salad, 18
Sautéed summer squash, 86
Green salad Caroline, 97
Cheese cake, 35
Fresh cherries
Demitasse

California Pinot Chardonnay

THANKSGIVING DINNER

Oysters on the half shell
California Pinot Chardonnay

Roast turkey with corn bread and pecan stuffing, 71
Sweet-potato soufflé, 70
Quick green beans, 157
Creamed onions
California Pinot Noir

Cranberry pie, 137
Café brûlot, 102

CHRISTMAS DINNER

Dry sherry   Walnut canapés, 131

Oysters on the half shell
Roast goose with corn bread and fruit stuffing, 143
Onion soufflé, 115
Buttered green peas
Peppermint-stick ice cream, 215
Christmas-wreath cookies, 65
Demitasse

Champagne

Menu Planner

❦

The recipe index which follows is designed to serve as a menu planner as well as to locate recipes by name. The entries therefore include the following categories:

224

Recipe Index

❧

Almond cakes, Chinese, 49
Ambrosia, 109
  Hawaiian, 187
Apple(s)
  baked ham with, 141
  brown Betty, 85
  pie, open maple, 203
  Vermont baked, 17
Asparagus and ham in cheese sauce,
    133
Avocado(es)
  cream Sturgis, 88
  cream of, soup, 5
  in *guacamole*
  stuffed, 158

Baking powder biscuits, 142
Barbecued duck, orange, 7
  lamb, mint, 104
  spareribs, 182
  steak, rock salt, 37
Bass (striped), baked stuffed, 28
Batter cakes, Susan Rockey's corn-
    meal, 192
  bread, 43
Beans, *see* Casseroles; Salads; Soups;
    Vegetables

BEEF
  Beef, boiled, and cream horseradish
    sauce, 47

BEEF, *Cont.*
  —, Stroganoff, 72
  Hamburgers, glorified, 166
  Red flannel hash, 132
  Sirloin, broiled, with blue cheese, 44
  Steak and kidney pie, 80
  —, Barry Wall, 59
  —, rock salt barbecued, 37

Beets, *see* Vegetables
Benné biscuits, Charleston, 23
Bethany, baked hen, 111

BEVERAGES
  Café brûlot, 102
  Farewell punch, 169
  Ginger-ale julep, 205

Biscuits, *see* Breads & Baking
Bisque, shrimp and oyster, 120
Blintzes, cheese, 118
Blueberry pie, open, 26
Bong Choy's, Mrs., Korean chicken,
    147
Borsch, 87
Bouillon, clam and tomato, 191
Bread, sauce, for pheasant, 209
  and cheese charlotte, 196

BREADS & BAKING (*see also* Cakes;
    Cookies; Pies)
  Biscuits, baking powder, 142

225

226

Cookies:
Chinese almond cakes, 49
Christmas-wreath cookies, 65
Cream pralines, 162
Coq au vin, California, 186
Corn, *see* Soups; Vegetables
Corn bread, *see* Stuffings
Corn-meal batter cakes, Susan
Rockey's, 192
Country captain, 25
Crab, *see* Shellfish
Cranberry(ies)
ham steak with, 16
pie, 137
sauce deluxe, June Platt's
Croquettes, sweet-potato, 48
turkey-hominy, Miss Parloa's, 94
Cucumber soup, iced, 199
Curried chicken in cream, 188
lobster in cream, 206
veal stew, 152
Curry, international lamb, 57

DESSERTS
Ambrosia, 109
Hawaiian, 187
Apple brown Betty, 85
Apples, Vermont baked, 17
Avocado cream Sturgis, 88
Cheese cake, 35
Chocolate icebox mousse, 19
Filbert pudding, 69
Ice, tropical, 82
Ice cream, peppermint-stick, 215
—, Philadelphia peach, 55
—, cake, pumpkin, 113
Indian pudding, 54
Lemon sponge, 46
Maple foamy sauce, 144
Mocha rum soufflé, 126
Orange cream charlotte, 156
Pie, cranberry, 137
—, French-silk, 146
—, lemon chess, 153
—, open blueberry, 26
—, open maple apple, 203
—, Southern pecan, 29

DESSERTS, *Cont.*
—, sweet potato, 184
Raspberries and whipped cream
cheese, 68
Rhubarb crumble, 114
Seedless grapes in cream, 161
Strawberry mousse, 53

Diat, Vichyssoise, 34
Dressing, French, 18
Dressings, *see* Stuffings
Duck, *see* Game; Poultry

Eggplant, *see* Vegetables
Egg sauce, for salmon, 181

EGGS (*see also* Soufflé)
Eggs foo yung, 13
—, goldenrod stuffed, 52
—, herb garden baked, 116
—, in hell, 66
—, scalloped, and onions, 56
—, shirred, with caper sauce, 20
—, Sunday, Sheeline, 170
Golden Buck, 84
Hangtown fry, 155
Omelette Roger Machell, 117
—, smoked-salmon, 21

Emerson bread, 76

Farewell punch, 169
Filbert pudding, 69

FISH (*see also* Shellfish)
Bass (striped) baked stuffed, 28
Catfish court-bouillon, 129
Cioppino, 127
Codfish cakes, 112
Fish chowder, Spite House, 62
—, savory broiled, 176
Flounder, baked, with minced clams,
202
Pompano, Royal Poinciana stuffed,
74
Rockfish, baked stuffed, 28

FISH, *Cont.*
Salmon, Fourth of July, 181
— kedgeree, 32
— trout, baked, 42
—, smoked, omelette, 21
Shad roe, golden-fried, 214
Trout, chilled poached, 90
Whitefish, planked Lake Michigan, 8

Flounder, baked, with minced clams, 202
Frankfurters, cocktail, in wine, 210
French dressing, 18
French-silk pie, 146

GAME
Duck, roast wild, 41
Pheasant, roast, 24
—, roast, with bread sauce, 209
Rock Cornish game birds, braised, 11
—, with mushrooms, 159
Venison stew, red wine, 136
Wild-rice stuffing for game birds, 107

Gazpacho, 122
Golden buck, 84
Goose, roast, with corn bread and fruit stuffing, 143
Grand Central oyster stew, 201
Grapes, seedless, in cream, 161
Guacamole, 67

HAM & PORK
Ham à la King, 79
—, asparagus and, in cheese sauce, 133
—, baked country-cured, 207
—, pie, jellied veal and, 165
—, steaks with cranberries, 16
—, with apples, baked, 141
Pork chops, stuffed, 160
—, with apples, 45
Sausage meat, homemade, 36
Spareribs, barbecued, 182

Hangtown fry, 155
Hamburgers, glorified, 166
Hash, red flannel, 132
Hominy, croquettes, Miss Parloa's turkey, 94
soufflé, 148
Hors-d'oeuvre, *see* Cocktail Hors-d'oeuvre
Horseradish, cream sauce, for beef, 47

Ice cream, *see* Desserts
Indian pudding, 54

Jambalaya, shrimp, 171
Jelly, fresh mint, 61
Jonny cakes, Rhode Island, 78
Julep, ginger-ale, 205

Kasha, 106
Kedgeree, salmon, 32
Kerr, Alvin, spiced tomatoes, 212
Ketchup, mushroom, 89
Kidneys, *see* Meats, Misc.

LAMB
Lamb curry, international, 57
—, mint-barbecued, 104
—, roast leg of, with mint sauce, 185
Mock venison (marinated roast leg of lamb), 164

Lemon sponge, 46
chess pie, 153
Lettuce and scallion soup, 103
Liptauer, 149
Lobster, *see* Shellfish

Machell, Roger, omelette, 117
Maple syrup, in
apple pie, open, 203
foamy sauce, 144
icing, 177
Vermont baked apples, 177
Matzo balls, chicken soup with, 108

Soufflé (*see also* Batter Bread)
  hominy, 148
  mocha rum, 126
  onion, 115
  sweet potato, 70

SOUPS
  Borsch, 87
  Clam and tomato bouillon, 191
  Fish chowder, Spite House, 62
  Gazpacho, 122
  Oyster stew, Grand Central, 201
  Shrimp and oyster bisque, 120
  Soup, avocado, cream of, 5
  —, bean, U. S. Senate, 3
  —, chicken, with matzo balls, 108
  —, chicken, with potato puffs, 150
  —, cream of fresh tomato, with dill, 145
  —, green corn, 96
  —, iced cucumber, 199
  —, lettuce and scallion, 103
  Vichyssoise Diat, 34

Spareribs, barbecued, 182
Spinach, Chinese, 91
Spite House fish chowder, 62
Squab in sauerkraut, 75
Squash, sautéed summer, 86
Squire, casserole, 81
Steak, *see* Beef; Ham

STEWS
  California *coq au vin,* 186
  Catfish court-bouillon, 129
  Cioppino, 127
  Country captain, 25
  Stew, kidney, 216
  —, lobster, 31
  —, oyster, Grand Central, 201
  —, veal, curried, 152
  —, venison, red wine, 136

Strawberry mousse, 53
Stuffings:
  Corn bread, and fruit, for goose, 143
    and pecan, for turkey, 71

Stuffings, *Cont.*
  Rice, spiced, for chicken, 204
    wild, for duck and game birds, 107
  Sturgis, avocado cream, 88
  Sweet potato, *see* Pies; Vegetables

Taffy, salt-water, 134
Tamale pie, 101
Tart, cheese and olive, 178
Tomato (*see also* Soups)
  pickle, green, 12
Tomaotes Alvin Kerr, spiced, 212
Tongue, boiled, with raisin sauce, 93
Tropical ice, 82
Trout, chilled poached, 90
  salmon, baked, 42
Turnovers, deviled ham, 163

U. S. Senate bean soup, 3

VEAL
  Veal and ham pie, jellied, 165
  — chops in sour cream, 211
  —, minced, in cream, 64
  — stew, curried, 152

VEGETABLES (*see also* Salads)
  Asparagus and ham in cheese sauce, 133
  Beans, quick green, 157
    (*see also* Casseroles; Salads; Soups)
  Beets, simmered, 173
  —, Yale, 2
  Brussels sprouts, glazed, 167
  Cabbage, quick creamed, 183
  — rolls, Swedish, 95
  Colache, 99
  Corn, baked green, 83
  — oysters, 39
  Eggplant, broiled, with parsley butter, 174
    with clam stuffing, 77
  Kasha, 106
  Mushrooms, flamed, in cream, 130